From Ground to Cloud

Cloud

Transforming IT with Intune

Dr. Patrick Jones

OLYMPUS ACADEMY
PRESS

Table of Contents

The Blueprint

Alex adjusted his headset and sat back in his chair, staring at the three glowing monitors on his desk. It was 9:00 a.m., and his calendar blinked with the reminder: Kickoff Call – Intune Project for 365 Strategies. He took a deep breath, scanning the detailed scope of work document he'd spent the weekend reviewing. Setting up Microsoft Intune and Autopilot for three separate tenants in a hybrid Active Directory environment was ambitious. It was one of those projects that could either make or break the quarter—and Alex wasn't about to let it break.

But this wasn't just a technical challenge; it was a puzzle, layered with interdependencies, multiple stakeholders, and the tight timelines Alex had grown accustomed to. As the senior IT strategist at 365 Strategies, he knew the stakes. This project wasn't just about delivering a service—it was about redefining how the organization managed devices, apps, and security in an increasingly complex, hybrid work world.

The ringtone broke his train of thought. It was time to begin.

The meeting began with introductions. Representing 365 Strategies, Alex led the call alongside IT Operations Manager Rachel, who would be his counterpart for internal coordination. On the client side, three tenant administrators joined the call, each responsible for one of the company's global regions. Their job: provide the ground-level details Alex needed to unify their device management under one cohesive plan. Also on the call were two directors—one from Security and another from Operations—tasked with ensuring compliance and functionality didn't clash.

"Thanks, everyone, for joining," Alex started. "This is going to be a complex but rewarding project, and I want us to stay aligned on every milestone. Let's go over the deliverables and expectations so we can hit the ground running."

Alex pulled up the project plan and shared his screen. The words Project Initiation appeared at the top, followed by a neatly organized timeline of milestones: initiation, discovery, configuration, testing, and deployment.

His voice was calm but clear as he walked through the objectives:

- Introduce stakeholders and finalize the project plan.
- Collect detailed information about existing infrastructure and devices.
- Develop configurations for Intune, Autopilot, and Conditional Access across all three tenants.
- Ensure every device, app, and VPN setting works seamlessly before deployment.

While the scope was massive, Alex was careful to break it down into digestible steps. Each tenant had its quirks, but those would come into focus during the discovery phase. For now, it was about creating a blueprint for success.

"Let's talk device naming conventions and app deployment plans," Alex prompted. He knew from experience that the smallest detail—like a poorly chosen naming scheme—could cascade into chaos during deployment.

The tenant admins chimed in one by one. Region A wanted a straightforward alphanumeric scheme based on location and department. Region B needed device names tied to compliance labels. Region C, to Alex's amusement, didn't yet have a preference.

"Great," Alex said, typing furiously into his notes. "We'll consolidate these into a unified standard that works for all tenants. Rachel and I will follow up with a draft naming convention after the call."

As the meeting went on, the scope grew sharper. VPN configurations would need to account for different regional access policies. Core applications had to be deployed globally, but certain apps—like the HR system in Region C—required localization. And of course, Conditional

Access policies had to ensure airtight security while remaining flexible enough for hybrid work scenarios.

As the call wound down, Alex felt the familiar thrill of diving into a large-scale project. He'd need to navigate complex infrastructure, streamline workflows, and solve unexpected roadblocks—likely at the least convenient moments. But those challenges were what made projects like this worthwhile.

"I'll send out today's notes and a finalized project plan for your review by tomorrow morning," Alex concluded. "Our next step will be the discovery phase, where we'll need detailed input on existing configurations and an inventory of devices. Once we have that, we'll dive into the design and setup stages. Any questions before we wrap up?"

After answering a few clarifying questions, Alex ended the call and exhaled. The real work was just beginning.

Notes:

This episode introduces Alex, the project, and the scope of work involved in setting up Intune and Autopilot across three tenants in a hybrid Active Directory environment. The kickoff meeting is a critical step in any IT project. It sets the stage for communication, alignment, and understanding of the deliverables.

Some key takeaways from this episode include:

- The importance of a well-structured project initiation phase to align stakeholders and clarify expectations.

- Breaking down large projects into manageable milestones helps teams stay focused.

- Even minor details, like device naming conventions, can significantly impact a project's success.

Charting New Territory

Alex stood in the break room of the 365 Strategies office, refilling his water bottle and scanning the whiteboard someone had scribbled with motivational quotes. One stood out: *"The biggest challenge in life is being yourself in a world trying to make you like everyone else."* He chuckled under his breath. It felt oddly fitting, given the project he was working on.

His current client was a multinational company that was stuck in an era of outdated on-premises systems, relying on Group Policy Objects (GPOs) and manual VPN setups to manage their devices. They didn't just need a solution—they needed an evolution. They'd contracted 365 Strategies to bring modern device management to life, building Microsoft Intune environments from the ground up. Alex knew this was no ordinary project. It was an opportunity to redefine how the client's IT department functioned while showing their leadership the value of forward-thinking technology.

At 365 Strategies, that was the mission: helping organizations across the country modernize their IT environments in ways that felt practical, approachable, and achievable. Alex's role as a Cloud Strategy Director wasn't just about implementation; it was about bridging the gap between possibility and reality. He'd been with the company for over four years and thrived on projects like this—where the stakes were high, the timelines were tight, and the payoff was transformative.

Back at his desk, Alex set his water bottle down and reviewed the day's schedule. He had three discovery calls lined up, each with one of the client's regional IT administrators. Each region had its own quirks and priorities, and Alex's goal was to uncover the details he'd need to design a unified yet flexible Intune environment.

He grabbed his notebook—a battered leather-bound journal he swore made him more organized than any app ever could—and dialed into his first call of the day.

Miguel, the admin for Region A, was waiting on the line. Alex had already reviewed some of Miguel's notes from the kickoff meeting, and he appreciated how thorough they were. Region A's setup was as traditional as it got: Windows devices managed entirely through GPOs, with little to no integration with cloud services.

"Good morning, Miguel. Thanks for hopping on," Alex began.

"Morning, Alex. I've got the inventory list you asked for—should I send it over now?" Miguel's voice was brisk, and Alex could tell he was someone who liked structure and predictability.

"That'd be great," Alex said. "And while you're at it, can you walk me through your current setup? I want to get a sense of what's working, what's not, and what your biggest concerns are."

Miguel launched into a detailed explanation of Region A's device management strategy—or lack thereof. They had about 1,500 devices, all managed through on-premises AD. VPN access was manual, requiring users to enter credentials each time, and app deployments were handled by scripts Miguel had written years ago.

"It works," Miguel concluded, "but it's not exactly efficient."

Alex smiled. "That's where Intune comes in. The goal is to take everything you're doing manually—provisioning, app deployments, security policies—and automate as much of it as possible. You'll still have control, but it'll save you a ton of time."

Miguel hesitated. "I like the idea of automation, but my team's not used to this kind of system. Is the learning curve going to be steep?"

"Not with the right plan," Alex assured him. "Part of my job is to make sure your team feels confident using Intune. We'll start small, build incrementally, and make sure you're comfortable every step of the way."

Priya, the admin for Region B, was next. Unlike Miguel, she had some experience with modern device management tools. While the company hadn't adopted Intune, Priya's region had experimented with third-party MDM solutions for their mobile devices.

"Hi, Priya. How's everything going?" Alex greeted her warmly.

"Busy, as usual," Priya replied with a laugh. "But I'm excited about this project. We've been needing something like Intune for a while now."

"That's great to hear," Alex said. "Tell me a bit about what you've tried in the past and where you're running into challenges."

Priya explained that their previous MDM solution had been clunky and difficult to integrate with their existing systems. It worked well enough for managing mobile devices, but it didn't extend to their Windows laptops or desktops. Worse, it lacked the robust security features they needed, like Conditional Access.

"What we need," Priya concluded, "is something that works for everyone—whether they're in the office or working remotely. And Conditional Access is a big one for us. We've had a few scares with unauthorized access, so tightening that up is a top priority."

Alex nodded. "Conditional Access will be a game-changer for you. We'll make sure it's set up to enforce compliance across all devices, whether they're corporate-owned or BYOD."

Priya grinned. "I like the sound of that."

The final call of the day was with Ethan, the admin for Region C. Ethan's region was smaller than the others, with just a few hundred devices, but it was also the least mature in terms of IT infrastructure. Most of their devices weren't even domain-joined, and there was no centralized management system in place.

"Hey, Ethan. Thanks for taking the time to chat," Alex began.

"Of course," Ethan replied. "Though I should warn you—we're pretty behind compared to the other regions. I'm not sure how much help I'll be."

"Don't worry," Alex said. "Starting from scratch has its advantages. We can build something that fits your needs perfectly, without having to undo a lot of legacy configurations."

Ethan seemed to relax. "That's good to hear. Honestly, we're just excited to have a system that works. Right now, everything feels so... fragmented."

"We'll fix that," Alex promised. "The goal is to give you a centralized system where you can manage all your devices, apps, and policies from one place. It'll make your life a lot easier."

By the time Alex wrapped up his calls, his notebook was filled with pages of notes. Each region had its own challenges, but there were common threads: a reliance on manual processes, a lack of centralized management, and a desire for greater security and efficiency.

As he organized his notes, Alex couldn't help but reflect on how far 365 Strategies had come since he joined. The company had started as a small consultancy, helping local businesses adopt cloud technologies. Over the years, it had grown into a national leader in IT strategy, known for its ability to make complex projects feel manageable. For Alex, the work was more than just a job—it was a chance to make a real difference in how companies operated.

Notes:

This episode highlights the discovery phase of the project, where Alex begins to uncover the unique challenges and opportunities of building an Intune environment from scratch. Discovery isn't just about technical details—it's about understanding the people, processes, and culture behind the technology.

Key takeaways:

- Starting with no existing Intune setup offers a clean slate but requires careful planning to align with organizational goals.

- Each region's unique challenges must be addressed while maintaining a unified approach.

- Building trust and confidence with stakeholders is essential for a successful transition.

Designing the Framework

The early morning sunlight filtered through Alex's office window as he powered up his workstation. A steaming mug of coffee sat within arm's reach, its rich aroma mingling with the faint hum of his desktop tower. The discovery phase was complete, and the real work was about to begin: designing a comprehensive Intune environment from scratch.

This was the part of the process Alex loved most—taking a sea of notes, technical quirks, and stakeholder expectations and transforming them into a coherent plan. For Alex, it wasn't just about solving technical problems. It was about crafting a framework that empowered the organization, turning what felt like an insurmountable challenge into a manageable, step-by-step strategy.

Alex leaned back in his chair, revisiting the notes from the three regional discovery sessions. Each region had its nuances, but the commonalities were clear:

- **Region A** relied heavily on on-premises Active Directory with Group Policy Objects (GPOs) controlling their devices.

- **Region B** had dipped its toes into modern management with third-party tools, but their infrastructure was fragmented.

- **Region C** was starting from scratch, with no centralized management system in place.

It was clear that this organization needed a clean slate to move into the cloud. The first order of business was to design an Intune tenant for each region, standardizing core configurations while allowing for regional flexibility where needed.

Alex began drafting the high-level framework:

1. **Tenant Setup**
   - Configure Microsoft Intune in each tenant to align with the organization's Microsoft 365 ecosystem.

- Establish baseline policies that could be customized for regional needs.

2. **Device Management Framework**

   - Design policies for device compliance, application deployment, and security baselines.

   - Develop Conditional Access policies to enforce secure access across all regions.

3. **Deployment Strategy**

   - Create and test Autopilot profiles to streamline provisioning for new devices.

   - Establish a rollout plan for migrating existing devices to Intune management.

4. **User Training and Documentation**

   - Prepare resources to train IT admins and end users, ensuring a smooth transition.

The phone buzzed on Alex's desk, pulling him from his thoughts. It was Rachel, the IT Operations Manager, calling to confirm a few details.

"Morning, Alex. How are things coming along?"

"Good morning! I'm just starting on the design phase. Wanted to check with you—has the leadership team decided how they want to handle tenant-level permissions?" Alex asked.

"We've been discussing it," Rachel replied. "The idea is to have a core IT team with admin access to all three tenants, but regional admins will manage day-to-day tasks."

"Perfect," Alex said. "That gives us a clear structure. I'll configure tenant admin roles to reflect that hierarchy."

Rachel paused. "What about shared policies? Should we have one baseline policy for all regions, or let each region create their own?"

Alex thought for a moment. "We'll do both. I'll set up global policies for things like device compliance and Conditional Access, but regions will have the flexibility to create their own app deployment and VPN configurations."

"Sounds good," Rachel said. "Let me know if you need anything else."

With the tenant setup plan finalized, Alex shifted his focus to policy design. This was where the real customization happened. He started by drafting a list of core policies that would serve as the foundation for all three regions:

1. **Device Compliance Policy**

   o Require encryption on all devices.

   o Enforce password complexity standards.

   o Ensure devices are running the latest OS version.

2. **Conditional Access Policy**

   o Block access from personal devices unless they meet compliance standards.

   o Require MFA for all users accessing corporate resources.

3. **Security Baselines**

   o Enable Microsoft Defender across all managed devices.

   o Restrict administrative privileges on endpoint devices.

Once the core policies were outlined, Alex created placeholders for regional-specific policies. For example:

- **Region A** needed localized app deployment for HR and logistics tools.

- **Region B** required hybrid support for BYOD users.

- **Region C** needed VPN configurations to support remote access for employees in rural areas.

Next, Alex turned his attention to Autopilot. The discovery phase had revealed significant inefficiencies in the client's current device provisioning process. Autopilot offered a way to automate and simplify the setup of new devices, making them ready for use right out of the box.

He began by drafting Autopilot profiles for each region:

1. **Region A Profile**

   o Standard naming conventions based on location and department.

   o Pre-installed apps, including Office 365 and Adobe Creative Cloud.

2. **Region B Profile**

   o Configurations for both corporate-owned and BYOD devices.

   o Pre-installed VPN client for accessing on-prem resources.

3. **Region C Profile**

   o Minimalist setup to support their smaller, simpler infrastructure.

   o VPN auto-connect enabled through Intune policies.

Alex made a note to schedule a meeting with the regional admins to review the profiles and ensure they met each region's needs.

By late afternoon, Alex had a draft of the design framework ready. It was an ambitious plan, but it was also achievable. He sent a copy to Rachel for feedback, along with a note:

Hi Rachel,

Here's the initial draft of the Intune design framework. Let me know if you or the regional admins have any questions or suggestions. Once we finalize this, we can move into the configuration phase.

Best,
Alex

Satisfied, Alex leaned back in his chair and took a deep breath. The design phase was always the most intellectually demanding, but it was also the most rewarding. With the framework in place, the next steps—building and testing the configurations—would feel like laying bricks on a foundation he'd carefully crafted.

Notes:

In this episode, Alex transitions from discovery to design, crafting the framework for a modern Intune environment. This phase is where the project's vision takes shape, balancing global policies with regional flexibility.

Key takeaways:

- **Tenant Setup:** Establishing clear administrative roles and permissions is critical for managing complex environments.

- **Policy Design:** Core policies provide a unified foundation, while regional-specific policies address unique needs.

- **Autopilot Profiles:** Automating device provisioning streamlines IT workflows and improves end-user experiences.

Getting Started with Tenant A: Device Enrollment Demystified

The soft click of the mouse echoed through Alex's quiet office as he navigated to the Devices section in the Microsoft Endpoint Manager Admin Center. For Tenant A, this was where it all began: enrolling devices into Intune. Without this foundational step, none of the compliance policies, app deployments, or Conditional Access rules would have any effect. Device enrollment was the gateway to cloud management, a bridge between the organization's on-premises setup and its modern future.

But device enrollment wasn't just a technical task; it was a strategic decision. Alex needed to ensure the process was secure, efficient, and scalable—qualities that would give Miguel's IT team confidence in their new system. With his notes and coffee in hand, Alex got to work.

Before diving into the technical steps, Alex reflected on why enrollment mattered so much. For organizations like Tenant A, enrollment served three critical purposes:

1. **Centralized Management:** Enrollment allowed Tenant A's IT team to manage all devices—whether they were in the office or remote—from a single interface.

2. **Security:** By enrolling devices into Intune, the IT team could enforce compliance rules, such as requiring encryption and strong passwords, to protect corporate data.

3. **Automation:** Enrollment paved the way for features like Autopilot and automatic app deployment, reducing manual effort and streamlining IT workflows.

Alex started by enabling automatic enrollment, a feature that linked devices joined to Azure AD directly to Intune. This was the most efficient way to ensure that devices were brought under management as soon as they were added to the organization's directory.

1. In the Endpoint Manager portal, Alex navigated to Devices > Enroll Devices > Automatic Enrollment.

2. He toggled the setting to enable automatic enrollment for all hybrid Azure AD joined devices.

3. Alex set permissions to allow Miguel's IT team to monitor and manage enrollment logs.

Automatic enrollment eliminates the need for IT staff to manually add each device to Intune, saving time and ensuring consistency. It also ensures that only devices authenticated through Azure AD can enroll, reducing the risk of rogue devices accessing corporate resources.

Tenant A's leadership had emphasized the importance of controlling which devices could enroll in Intune. To meet this requirement, Alex configured enrollment restrictions, a feature that blocked personal devices and required all enrolled devices to be pre-approved.

1. Alex created a device type restriction policy to block personal devices from enrolling in Intune.

2. He added a device limit restriction, ensuring that each user could enroll no more than five devices.

3. To enforce pre-approval, Alex worked with Miguel to generate a list of approved device IDs from their asset management system. These IDs were added to Intune's device identifiers list, creating a digital "allowlist."

Restricting enrollment ensures that only corporate-owned devices, which are already tracked and managed by Tenant A, can access the system. This step prevents personal devices, which may not meet security standards, from jeopardizing the organization's data.

As Alex enabled enrollment policies, he encountered a familiar challenge: legacy devices. About 200 devices in Tenant A's inventory were running older operating systems, primarily Windows 7. These devices couldn't be enrolled in Intune without significant updates or workarounds.

Alex's Plan for Legacy Devices:

1. **Upgrade Eligible Devices:** Alex identified devices capable of running Windows 10 and outlined a process for Miguel's team to upgrade them.

2. **Document the Upgrade Process:** He drafted a guide on using Intune's Update Management feature to automate future OS updates.

3. **Phased Rollout:** For devices that couldn't be upgraded immediately, Alex recommended a phased approach, upgrading 20–30 devices at a time to minimize disruption.

Legacy devices pose a risk not only to operational efficiency but also to security. Addressing these devices early ensures a smoother transition and prevents potential vulnerabilities.

With the enrollment policies configured, Alex moved on to testing—a critical step to ensure everything worked as expected before rolling it out to the full device inventory.

1. **Create a Test Group:** Alex created an Azure AD group called Tenant A Test Devices and added five test devices to it.

2. **Run Enrollment Scenarios:** Alex tested several scenarios to validate the enrollment process:

   o **Scenario 1:** Enrolling a compliant device.

   o **Scenario 2:** Attempting to enroll a non-compliant device (e.g., running an unsupported OS).

   o **Scenario 3:** Attempting to enroll an unapproved device.

3. **Monitor Logs:** Alex monitored the enrollment logs in Endpoint Manager, ensuring each scenario produced the expected results.

Test Results:

- The compliant device enrolled successfully, applying the baseline compliance policy automatically.

- The non-compliant device was flagged and blocked from enrolling.

- The unapproved device failed to enroll, reinforcing the effectiveness of the allowlist.

Testing identifies potential issues before they impact the wider organization. It ensures that the enrollment process is robust, secure, and aligned with organizational policies.

By the end of the day, Alex had successfully configured and tested the enrollment process for Tenant A. He sent a summary email to Miguel:

Hi Miguel,

The enrollment policies for Tenant A are now live and functioning as expected. Test devices have successfully enrolled, and the restriction settings are working to block unauthorized devices.

Here's what's next:

- *We need to finalize the upgrade plan for legacy devices.*

- *I recommend starting enrollment with your newer devices in batches to ensure a smooth rollout.*

Let me know if you encounter any issues or have additional questions.

Best,
Alex

Notes:

This episode breaks down the critical steps in setting up device enrollment for Tenant A, emphasizing both the how and the why behind each configuration. Enrollment is the foundation of any Intune environment, and understanding these steps ensures a smooth and secure transition.

Key takeaways:

- **Automatic Enrollment:** Simplifies management by automatically adding devices to Intune upon Azure AD join.

- **Enrollment Restrictions:** Protects organizational data by ensuring only approved devices can enroll.

- **Legacy Devices:** Addressing outdated hardware early prevents future complications.

- **Testing:** Validating configurations with real-world scenarios is crucial for success.

Translating Legacy: Migrating GPOs to Intune for Tenant A

The glow of Alex's monitors illuminated his focused expression as he reviewed the Group Policy Analytics report he'd generated during the discovery phase. Tenant A was deeply rooted in Group Policy Objects (GPOs), using them to manage nearly every aspect of their 1,500-device environment. Migrating these policies to Intune wasn't just a task—it was a transformation.

For Alex, this step was about more than technical execution. It was about bridging the gap between a traditional on-premises approach and the flexibility of modern cloud-based management. The stakes were high; the policies needed to work seamlessly in Intune, or risk disrupting workflows across Tenant A's entire operation.

He leaned forward, rolling up his sleeves. This was where experience met creativity.

GPOs are the backbone of many traditional IT environments, controlling everything from user permissions to software settings. For Tenant A, these policies had grown over the years into a sprawling web of rules—some essential, some outdated, and others redundant.

Migrating these policies into Intune served three key purposes:

1. **Centralization:** Intune allowed Tenant A to manage policies alongside device compliance and app deployments in a single interface.

2. **Simplification:** Intune's streamlined policy management reduced the complexity of maintaining hundreds of GPOs.

3. **Flexibility:** Unlike GPOs, Intune policies worked seamlessly across hybrid and remote environments.

Alex began by revisiting the Group Policy Analytics report he'd created earlier. This tool, available in Microsoft Endpoint Manager, was designed to evaluate existing GPOs and determine their compatibility with Intune.

1. Alex exported Tenant A's GPOs from their on-premises Active Directory environment.

2. He uploaded the export file to the Group Policy Analytics section in Endpoint Manager.

3. The tool generated a report categorizing the GPOs into three groups:

    o **Supported Policies:** Fully compatible with Intune.

    o **Partially Supported Policies:** Require modifications before they can be implemented in Intune.

    o **Unsupported Policies:** Cannot be migrated and may require alternative solutions.

What the Report Revealed:

- 60% of Tenant A's GPOs were fully supported by Intune.

- 25% were partially supported and needed adjustments.

- 15% were unsupported, including some legacy settings no longer relevant to the organization.

Not all GPOs were created equal, and Alex knew that focusing on the most impactful policies first would yield the best results. He categorized the GPOs into three priority levels:

1. **High Priority:** Security-related policies, such as password requirements, BitLocker encryption, and administrative permissions.

2. **Medium Priority:** User experience policies, such as desktop settings and browser configurations.

3. **Low Priority:** Policies with minimal impact or those scheduled for deprecation.

Alex started with the high-priority policies. These were critical for ensuring compliance and protecting Tenant A's sensitive data.

With his priorities set, Alex began creating equivalent policies in Intune for the high-priority GPOs. He navigated to the Configuration Profiles section in Endpoint Manager, where he could create, assign, and manage policies.

Example: Password Policy

1. **GPO Equivalent:** Require complex passwords with a minimum of eight characters, including uppercase, lowercase, numbers, and symbols.

2. **Intune Configuration:** Alex created a Device Configuration Profile using the Windows 10 and later template. He set the password requirements to match the existing GPO.

3. **Assignment:** The policy was assigned to Tenant A's All Devices Azure AD group to ensure universal application.

Example: BitLocker Encryption

1. **GPO Equivalent:** Enable BitLocker encryption on all devices, requiring TPM 2.0 for security.

2. **Intune Configuration:** Alex created a Security Baseline Profile in Intune, enabling BitLocker and setting encryption methods to AES-256.

3. **Assignment:** This policy was applied to all compliant devices, with a separate alert configured for devices that failed to meet the encryption standard.

Example: Administrative Permissions

1. **GPO Equivalent:** Restrict administrative permissions to IT staff only.

2. **Intune Configuration:** Alex created a Local User Group Membership Policy, ensuring that only users in the IT Admins Azure AD group could have local admin rights.

As Alex created each policy, he tested it on a subset of devices from Tenant A's inventory to ensure it worked as intended.

How It's Done:

1. Alex added five test devices to a Pilot Group in Azure AD.

2. He applied the new Intune policies to the Pilot Group and monitored the results in the Endpoint Manager dashboard.

3. For each policy, Alex verified:

    o   The settings were applied correctly.

    o   No conflicts occurred with other policies.

    o   End-user workflows were unaffected.

Challenges and Adjustments:

*   **Issue:** The BitLocker policy failed on a test device without TPM 2.0.

*   **Solution:** Alex created an exception policy for older devices, enabling BitLocker without TPM while flagging them for replacement.

*   **Issue:** A legacy browser setting caused conflicts with Intune's compliance policies.

*   **Solution:** Alex updated the browser settings to match modern standards, resolving the conflict.

The final task was to address the 15% of GPOs that couldn't be migrated to Intune. Alex worked closely with Miguel to evaluate these policies and determine their relevance.

*   **Outdated Policies:** Many unsupported GPOs were legacy settings no longer needed. These were documented and removed.

*   **Third-Party Tools:** A few policies managed settings for third-party tools not integrated with Intune. Alex recommended

alternative solutions, such as deploying the tools via Intune's app deployment feature.

Unsupported GPOs can create gaps in policy enforcement if not properly addressed. By documenting and resolving these issues, Alex ensured that Tenant A's new system was both comprehensive and future-proof.

By the end of the day, Alex had migrated all high-priority GPOs into Intune, tested the configurations, and addressed the unsupported policies. He sent an update to Miguel:

Hi Miguel,

I've completed the migration of high-priority GPOs into Intune and tested them with a pilot group of devices. The results look great, and the policies are working as intended.

Next, we'll focus on medium-priority policies and begin scaling the rollout to more devices. Let me know if you'd like to review anything before we proceed.

Best,
Alex

Notes:

This episode explores the critical process of migrating Group Policy Objects (GPOs) into Intune, providing a step-by-step guide that balances technical details with practical insights.

Key takeaways:

- **Group Policy Analytics:** A powerful tool for identifying which GPOs are compatible with Intune.

- **Prioritization:** Focusing on high-impact policies ensures a smooth transition and immediate benefits.

- **Testing:** Running policies on a pilot group helps catch and resolve issues early.

- **Unsupported Policies:** Evaluating and addressing gaps ensures no critical settings are overlooked.

Refining the Details: Medium-Priority Policies and User Experience

Alex stared at the task list on his screen, sipping his second cup of coffee for the day. The high-priority policies for Tenant A were complete, tested, and ready for deployment. Now it was time to tackle the medium-priority policies, those that shaped the user experience. These weren't about compliance or security—they were about usability, productivity, and ensuring that employees felt supported by the system rather than constrained by it.

Alex knew that while these policies didn't grab headlines like BitLocker encryption or password enforcement, they were just as important. A well-configured user experience could make or break the adoption of the new Intune environment.

For many organizations, a transition to modern management can feel disruptive. Policies that are too strict or poorly aligned with day-to-day workflows can frustrate employees and lead to resistance. The goal with these medium-priority policies was to create a system that was both secure and user-friendly, ensuring that employees experienced the benefits of Intune without unnecessary friction.

Tenant A's employees had grown used to customized desktop and start menu layouts configured via GPOs. Alex's task was to replicate these settings in Intune while allowing some degree of flexibility for users.

As Alex sat at his desk, he opened Microsoft Endpoint Manager, the hub for managing all the tenants' devices. He clicked through to the Configuration Profiles section, a part of the system that felt like the backbone of Intune. Each profile he created here acted as a blueprint, shaping how devices behaved for their users.

For Tenant A, the Start Menu layout was more than just a convenience—it was a familiar tool employees relied on to quickly access

29

their daily apps. Claire, Tenant A's IT Director, had been clear about their need to retain consistency as they transitioned to a modern management system. Key applications like Microsoft Teams, Outlook, and OneDrive needed to be front and center, just as employees had grown accustomed to.

Alex scrolled through the available options, selecting Windows 10 and later as the template for this configuration. The interface guided him step by step, presenting a range of customizable settings. Among them, Alex spotted the Start Menu Layout option—exactly what he was looking for.

He clicked into the settings, where he found a blank field prompting him to upload a configuration file. This would dictate the arrangement of tiles and shortcuts on the Start Menu. He made a mental note to revisit this step after preparing the file.

To mirror Tenant A's existing layout, Alex needed to create an XML file—a structured document that would define the Start Menu's organization. Drawing on his familiarity with similar setups, he opened a basic text editor and began crafting the file.

The process required precision. Each section of the XML file represented a tile or app grouping, and Alex carefully listed Tenant A's essential apps. He started with Microsoft Teams, defining its position as a large tile at the top-left corner of the menu. Below that, he placed Outlook, OneDrive, and a few other frequently used applications. Finally, he added a folder for utilities, grouping apps like the Calculator and Snipping Tool for easy access.

When the file was complete, Alex saved it as StartMenuLayout.xml and uploaded it to the Endpoint Manager portal.

Back in the Configuration Profiles section, Alex selected the option to upload the XML file. With a few clicks, the file was imported, and a preview displayed the new layout—a clean, organized Start Menu that mirrored what employees were used to seeing.

Satisfied with the setup, Alex assigned the profile to a test group within Tenant A. These devices would apply the configuration the next time they connected to Intune.

Alex picked up a test laptop and rebooted it to trigger the new configuration. As the device restarted, he watched the Start Menu refresh with the new layout. The tiles were perfectly arranged, with Teams and Outlook prominently displayed at the top.

"This is exactly what they needed," Alex thought. "A small change, but it will make a big difference in helping employees feel at home with their devices."

He documented the process carefully, knowing Claire's team might want to replicate it for future updates. After testing the profile on a handful of devices, Alex rolled it out to the rest of Tenant A, confident that this step would enhance productivity while easing the transition to Intune. A familiar desktop and start menu layout minimizes the learning curve for employees, making the transition smoother.

During testing, Alex realized that forcing a fixed layout prevented employees from adding their own shortcuts. To address this, he adjusted the policy to set a default layout while allowing customization.

Browser settings were another area where Tenant A relied heavily on GPOs. These policies ensured that employees used secure, standardized browsers configured with the necessary bookmarks and extensions.

Alex leaned forward, adjusting his monitor as he reviewed the list of requested customizations for Tenant A's new default browser: Microsoft Edge. Claire had recently overseen the switch to Edge, citing its tight integration with Microsoft 365 as a key advantage. Now, it was Alex's job to ensure the browser was set up to meet the organization's needs.

Tenant A's employees relied heavily on their company intranet, internal dashboards, and HR tools. To streamline their experience, Alex would configure Edge with a default homepage, preloaded bookmarks, and strict controls to prevent the use of unapproved browser extensions.

This would ensure consistency while improving security across the tenant.

Alex navigated to the Device Configuration Profiles section in Microsoft Endpoint Manager, a now-familiar territory where countless policies and settings were crafted. He clicked Create Profile and selected Windows 10 and later as the platform, opting for Administrative Templates as the settings type.

"Edge is flexible," Alex thought as he scrolled through the options. "But flexibility means complexity if you don't set clear boundaries."

He named the profile Tenant A - Microsoft Edge Configuration and began customizing the settings.

The first task was to configure the homepage. Claire had emphasized the importance of having the company intranet load automatically when employees opened Edge. Alex located the Set the homepage URL policy in the Administrative Templates.

He clicked the setting and entered the intranet URL: https://intranet.tenant-a.com

For good measure, he enabled the Prevent users from changing the homepage option, ensuring consistency across all devices. "This will make things easier for employees and reduce IT tickets," Alex thought, as he saved the changes.

Next, Alex tackled bookmarks. Tenant A relied on several internal tools, including HR software, finance dashboards, and project management portals. Preloading these bookmarks would save employees time and encourage the use of officially supported systems.

He located the Configure favorites setting and clicked Edit Policy. Using the format specified in Intune, Alex added the following bookmarks:

- **HR Tools**: https://hr.tenant-a.com
- **Finance Dashboard**: https://finance.tenant-a.com
- **Project Portal**: https://projects.tenant-a.com

He grouped these bookmarks under a folder named Tenant A Tools, ensuring they were neatly organized in the browser's favorites bar. "Employees shouldn't have to dig for what they need," Alex thought as he reviewed the configuration.

The last—and arguably most critical—task was to control browser extensions. While extensions could boost productivity, unapproved ones posed security risks. Alex found the Control which extensions cannot be installed policy and created a blocklist for known problematic extensions.

Additionally, he used the Allow specific extensions to be installed policy to pre-approve only the tools Claire's team had vetted, such as password managers and project management plugins.

To simplify IT management, Alex enabled the Prevent users from sideloading extensions policy, which blocked employees from installing extensions directly from their devices. "Better safe than sorry," he thought, as he saved the settings.

Satisfied with the setup, Alex assigned the profile to a pilot group of devices within Tenant A. He selected five laptops from different departments to ensure the policy worked across various roles.

On a test laptop, Alex launched Edge and watched as the homepage loaded instantly: the familiar interface of Tenant A's intranet. He opened the favorites bar and saw the neatly organized bookmarks. Lastly, he attempted to install a random extension, only to receive an error message:
"This extension has been blocked by your organization."

Everything worked perfectly.

With the pilot group successful, Alex deployed the Edge configuration profile to the rest of Tenant A's devices. He also prepared a brief training document for employees, explaining the new setup and highlighting the benefits of preloaded bookmarks and the controlled extensions policy.

Claire was thrilled with the results. "This is exactly the kind of user-friendly, secure experience we needed," she said during their follow-up meeting. Standardized browser settings ensure that employees can quickly access critical resources while maintaining security.

Some employees used third-party browsers for niche tasks. To accommodate them, Alex configured Conditional Access rules to ensure that sensitive resources were only accessible via compliant browsers.

Tenant A relied heavily on Microsoft 365 apps, and their previous GPOs had standardized settings for Word, Excel, and Outlook. Alex worked to replicate these configurations in Intune.

Alex stared at the Microsoft 365 apps dashboard, considering the potential impact of small, thoughtful configurations. These apps were the backbone of Tenant A's productivity, used daily for everything from drafting reports to managing projects. Claire had shared her vision: a streamlined experience where documents were auto-saved to OneDrive, email signatures reflected the company's branding, and employees had easy access to pre-configured templates in Word and Excel.

"This is about removing friction," Alex thought. "If everything just works, employees can focus on their work instead of figuring out settings."

Alex navigated to the Apps section in Microsoft Endpoint Manager and clicked App Configuration Policies. From here, he selected Add > Managed Apps, choosing Microsoft 365 Apps for Enterprise as the target.

He named the new policy Tenant A - Microsoft 365 Configuration and began tailoring the settings.

The first setting was a no-brainer: enabling auto-save to OneDrive for Business. This would ensure employees' work was continuously backed up, reducing the risk of lost files and encouraging collaboration.

Alex found the Save documents to OneDrive by default setting and toggled it on. To simplify things further, he configured OneDrive to save files to a company-specific folder structure:
Documents\Tenant A Work

"This will ensure everyone's work is in the right place, ready to share," Alex thought as he added the setting to the policy.

Next, Alex tackled email signatures. Claire wanted every outgoing email to reflect the company's branding, promoting a professional and unified image.

Alex uploaded a pre-designed HTML signature template that included:

- The employee's name, title, and department (auto-populated from Azure AD).

- Tenant A's logo and tagline.

- Contact information, including phone and email.

He used the Email Signature Setting within the policy to apply the template to all Outlook users. The system dynamically inserted user-specific details, ensuring each signature was personalized but consistent.

To test it, Alex assigned the policy to his account and sent himself a test email. The signature appeared perfectly formatted, with the logo neatly aligned and all fields auto-filled. "Professional and polished," he thought.

Alex's next task was setting up default templates in Word and Excel that adhered to Tenant A's branding guidelines. These templates included the company's logo, specific fonts, and pre-defined formatting styles.

He uploaded the templates to a shared OneDrive folder, ensuring they were centrally stored and easily updated by the design team.

In the configuration policy, Alex added the templates using the Default Templates Path setting. He set the path to: https://tenant-a-my.sharepoint.com/templates/

When users opened Word or Excel, the branded templates would now appear as the first options under the "New Document" menu.

Before deploying the policy to the entire tenant, Alex tested it on a small group of employees. He selected devices from different departments to ensure the settings worked across various roles.

1. **Auto-Save:** Alex opened Word on a test laptop, typed a few lines, and confirmed the document was automatically saved to the OneDrive path.

2. **Email Signatures:** He sent and received test emails from Outlook, verifying that the signatures were correctly applied.

3. **Templates:** Alex launched Word and Excel, confirming that the branded templates appeared in the default options.

While testing, Alex discovered a minor glitch: One employee's email signature wasn't populating their department information from Azure AD. After investigating, he found that the employee's department field in Azure AD was blank.

- Alex worked with Claire's team to audit Azure AD user attributes, ensuring all fields were populated correctly.

- He added a fallback rule to the signature template, inserting "Tenant A Employee" if any user-specific details were missing.

Satisfied with the results, Alex rolled out the configuration policy to all devices in Tenant A. The deployment was seamless, with most users noticing the changes immediately. To assist employees, Alex prepared a short guide explaining the new features, highlighting:

- How auto-save to OneDrive simplifies collaboration.

- The professional look of the new email signatures.

- The convenience of having pre-configured templates.

Pre-configured settings save employees time and ensure consistency across the organization.

By the end of the day, Alex felt confident that the medium-priority policies would enhance the user experience without introducing unnecessary complications. He sent a summary email to Miguel:

Hi Miguel,

The medium-priority policies are ready for deployment. We've tested them extensively with the pilot group and incorporated their feedback.

Here's the deployment plan:

- *Stage 1: IT staff and department heads.*

- *Stage 2: Full rollout in batches.*

Let's schedule a call to review the final settings before we proceed. Looking forward to hearing your thoughts!

Best,
Alex

Notes:

This episode focuses on the often-overlooked aspect of user experience policies, demonstrating how small details can significantly impact employee satisfaction and productivity.

Key takeaways:

- **Start Menu Layouts:** Default configurations should balance organizational needs with user flexibility.

- **Browser Settings:** Pre-configured bookmarks and compliant browser requirements streamline workflows and enhance security.

- **Office App Settings:** Tailored configurations save time and ensure consistency across teams.

- **Pilot Testing:** Involving employees in testing helps identify potential issues and build buy-in for the new system.

Scaling the Rollout: Tenant A Goes Live

The quiet hum of the office was broken only by the rhythmic tapping of Alex's keyboard as he prepared for the next phase of the project. It was time to take the carefully crafted policies for Tenant A and deploy them across the organization. This stage wasn't just about clicking "deploy" and walking away—it was about scaling thoughtfully, ensuring every configuration worked as intended, and preparing the IT team for what came next.

For Alex, this phase was where all the planning, testing, and adjustments came together. It was where the system stopped being an idea on paper and became the foundation for Tenant A's modern device management environment.

The rollout began with Miguel and his IT team. Before introducing the new Intune environment to the broader organization, Alex worked closely with them to ensure they were comfortable with the setup. Miguel had spent years managing devices through GPOs, and while he was excited about the shift to Intune, he admitted he still had some reservations.

"Change is always a little daunting," Miguel said during their morning call. "But I've got to say, the pilot group feedback has been encouraging."

Alex smiled. "That's exactly what we want. Let's focus on the first rollout group today and make sure everything works smoothly. Once you see it in action, I think you'll feel even more confident."

The first group to receive the new policies included Miguel's IT staff and a few department heads. This smaller, manageable group allowed Alex and Miguel to monitor the system's performance and troubleshoot any unexpected issues before rolling it out further.

The deployment process started with a quick check of the Configuration Profiles in Endpoint Manager. Each policy—from device compliance settings to the customized start menu layout—was assigned to a group in Azure AD. Alex double-checked that the assignments matched Miguel's preferences, ensuring each group received the correct configurations.

With everything in place, Alex initiated the deployment. Within minutes, devices in the IT and department head groups began syncing with Intune. Compliance policies enforced encryption and password standards, while application settings ensured employees had immediate access to the tools they needed.

As the devices synced, Alex and Miguel monitored the progress in real-time using the Device Compliance dashboard in Endpoint Manager. Most devices reported as compliant within minutes, but a handful flagged minor issues—primarily related to outdated operating systems.

"This is exactly why we start small," Alex said. "It's better to catch these now than during the full rollout."

Together, they addressed the flagged devices. For those running older OS versions, Alex applied a temporary exception policy, allowing them to sync while scheduling upgrades for a later date. For devices with missing encryption, he worked with Miguel's team to enable BitLocker manually.

Once the initial group was fully deployed and operational, Alex turned his attention to training Miguel's team. While the policies and configurations were now in place, the success of the system depended on the IT team's ability to manage and maintain it moving forward.

They spent the afternoon in a virtual training session, covering topics like:

- How to monitor compliance and resolve flagged devices.
- Adding new devices to the system.
- Adjusting policies for specific use cases.

Miguel's team asked thoughtful questions, and by the end of the session, Alex could see their confidence growing.

"This makes so much more sense now that we're seeing it in action," one of the team members said. "It's actually a lot easier than I expected."

The final phase of the day was preparing for the full rollout. Alex worked with Miguel to segment the remaining devices into manageable batches, scheduling deployments over the next several days. This staggered approach ensured that the IT team wouldn't be overwhelmed with support requests and allowed for quick adjustments if any issues arose.

Before signing off for the day, Alex sent Miguel a detailed rollout plan, including deployment schedules, troubleshooting tips, and a checklist for each phase.

Notes:

In this episode, Alex scales the deployment of Tenant A's Intune environment, taking the system live with a thoughtful, phased approach. This stage highlights the importance of collaboration, training, and flexibility during a rollout.

Key takeaways:

- Starting with a smaller group allows for real-time monitoring and issue resolution before scaling further.

- Collaboration with the IT team builds confidence and ensures a smoother transition.

- Staggered deployments reduce strain on IT resources and provide opportunities for adjustment.

Fine-Tuning the System: Post-Rollout Adjustments for Tenant A

The glow of the monitor reflected off Alex's glasses as he leaned in, scanning the Device Compliance dashboard in Microsoft Endpoint Manager. The initial rollout for Tenant A was complete, and most of the devices were now under Intune management. But Alex knew this phase wasn't the finish line—it was the start of fine-tuning. Even the most carefully planned deployments could reveal quirks once they were live at scale.

This was Alex's favorite part of the process: digging into the data, listening to feedback, and making the adjustments that turned a good system into a great one.

The first order of business was reviewing the compliance reports from the broader rollout. While the majority of devices reported as Compliant, a few flagged issues stood out. Alex categorized the flagged devices into three groups:

1. **Outdated Operating Systems:** Some devices were running older OS versions that didn't meet the compliance policy.

2. **Missing Encryption:** A handful of devices hadn't successfully enabled BitLocker.

3. **Conditional Access Issues:** A small number of users were blocked from accessing resources due to personal device usage or unapproved browsers.

Starting with the operating system issues, Alex identified the devices still running older versions of Windows. Most had been flagged during the initial pilot, but a few had slipped through the cracks during the full rollout. Alex reached out to Miguel to confirm the upgrade plan.

"Hey Miguel, I've got a list of devices that need OS updates. Should I push the updates through Intune, or would you prefer to handle it manually?"

Miguel replied quickly. "Let's use Intune. If we can automate it, we might as well."

Alex created an Update Compliance Policy in Intune, targeting the flagged devices and setting a schedule for after business hours to minimize disruption. Within minutes, the devices began downloading and installing the updates.

Next, Alex turned his attention to the devices missing encryption. Most of these were older machines that lacked the hardware support for automatic BitLocker activation. He adjusted the BitLocker policy to enable encryption for devices without TPM 2.0, applying a slightly lower standard for these legacy machines while flagging them for eventual replacement.

As the adjusted policy rolled out, Alex monitored its impact in the compliance dashboard. The number of non-compliant devices dropped steadily, giving him confidence that the tweaks were working.

The third challenge—Conditional Access issues—required a more nuanced approach. Many of the flagged users were attempting to access corporate resources from personal devices that hadn't been enrolled in Intune or approved through App Protection Policies.

To address this, Alex worked with Miguel to send a company-wide notification reminding employees about the updated access policies. The notification included:

- Steps for enrolling personal devices into Intune.
- Instructions for using approved browsers like Microsoft Edge.
- A contact email for IT support if employees encountered issues.

Within hours of the notification, several users had enrolled their devices or switched to compliant browsers. For those who needed additional help, Alex created a temporary Conditional Access exception group, allowing IT to manually approve access for users with urgent needs.

Beyond resolving flagged issues, Alex used this time to gather feedback from the employees and IT staff. During a scheduled call with Miguel's team, they shared their observations from the rollout.

"The start menu layout is a hit," one IT admin said. "But we've had a few people asking for more flexibility to pin their own apps."

Another admin added, "The compliance rules are working well, but a few employees have had trouble understanding why their devices are blocked. Maybe we could add more context to the error messages?"

Alex nodded, jotting down notes. "Great feedback. Let's tackle these one by one."

Based on the team's input, Alex made several refinements:

1. **Start Menu Customization:** He adjusted the start menu policy to allow more user customization while retaining the organizational defaults.

2. **Error Message Clarity:** Alex updated the compliance error messages to include specific instructions, such as "Your device is missing encryption. Contact IT for assistance."

3. **User-Friendly Documentation:** He created a short guide for employees, outlining common issues and how to resolve them.

The final step in the post-rollout phase was ensuring that Miguel's team was fully equipped to manage the system independently. Alex scheduled a follow-up training session focused on:

- Monitoring and resolving compliance issues.

- Adjusting policies as organizational needs evolved.

- Using Intune analytics to identify trends and plan future improvements.

During the session, one of Miguel's team members asked, "What happens if a device gets wiped or replaced? Do we have to start from scratch with the policies?"

Alex smiled. "Good question. That's where Windows Autopilot comes in. For any new or reset device, Autopilot will automatically apply all the configurations and policies as soon as it's enrolled. It's like hitting the reset button without losing any of your settings."

By the end of the week, Tenant A's Intune environment was running smoothly. The compliance rate was over 95%, user satisfaction was high, and Miguel's team felt confident in their ability to manage the system. Alex sent a final update to Miguel summarizing the progress:

Hi Miguel,

The post-rollout adjustments are complete, and I'm happy to report that Tenant A's Intune environment is now fully operational. Compliance rates are high, and we've addressed all flagged issues.

Thanks for your partnership on this project. Your team has done a fantastic job adapting to the new system. Let me know if there's anything else I can support you with as we move on to Tenant B.

Best,
Alex

Notes:

This episode focuses on the critical post-rollout phase, where Alex fine-tunes the system based on real-world feedback and prepares the IT team for long-term success.

Key takeaways:

- **Post-Rollout Adjustments:** Expect flagged issues and address them methodically to ensure stability.

- **Employee Communication:** Clear notifications and documentation help employees adapt to new policies.

- **Training and Empowerment:** Equipping the IT team ensures the system remains effective after deployment.

Laying the Groundwork for Tenant B: Managing BYOD

The glow of Alex's monitor reflected the complexity of the next step in the project: Tenant B's BYOD strategy. While Tenant A relied heavily on corporate-owned devices and traditional IT management, Tenant B embraced a more modern approach, allowing employees to use personal devices for work. The challenge for Alex wasn't just to secure these devices but to do so in a way that respected employees' privacy while ensuring corporate data remained protected.

BYOD environments were a balancing act, and Alex was determined to strike the right one. He took a sip of his coffee, opened the Endpoint Manager portal, and began reviewing his notes.

Tenant B's workforce was a mix of in-office and remote employees, with many relying on personal laptops, phones, and tablets to access company resources. Alex had identified several key goals during the discovery phase:

1. Protect corporate data within personal apps.

2. Create clear boundaries between personal and corporate usage.

3. Simplify the process for employees to enroll their devices.

To achieve these goals, Alex focused on configuring App Protection Policies (APPs)—a powerful feature in Intune designed specifically for BYOD scenarios.

Unlike traditional device management, which controls the entire device, APPs secure only the apps and data that belong to the organization. For example, corporate emails accessed through Outlook would be encrypted and protected, but photos, personal emails, and other apps on the same device would remain untouched.

This separation was critical for Tenant B, where employee privacy was a major concern. Alex knew that if employees felt their personal information was being monitored, they might resist adopting the new system.

Alex started by navigating to the Apps section in Microsoft Endpoint Manager and selecting App Protection Policies. He created a new policy targeting Android and iOS devices, as these were the most common personal devices used by Tenant B's workforce.

Tenant A had identified key apps—Outlook, Teams, OneDrive, and the Microsoft Office suite—as critical to daily operations. Alex's task was clear: configure these apps to ensure corporate data stayed secure, even on unmanaged devices.

"This is where security meets usability," Alex thought. "If I do this right, employees won't even notice the safeguards in place."

Alex navigated to the Apps section of Endpoint Manager and created a new App Protection Policy. The first decision was choosing the apps the policy would target. These were the core tools employees used for work:

- **Microsoft Outlook:** The hub for email and calendar management.

- **Microsoft Teams:** Tenant B's primary communication platform.

- **OneDrive:** Where employees stored and shared files.

- **Microsoft Word, Excel, and PowerPoint:** The go-to apps for productivity.

He added each app to the policy, ensuring they were flagged for data protection across both managed and unmanaged devices. This would allow Tenant B to extend security to employees using personal phones or tablets for work.

"Apps first," Alex murmured. "Then, we lock down the data."

The next step was setting up the safeguards that would govern how corporate data could be accessed, shared, and stored within the targeted apps.

1. Encrypting Data:

Alex enabled encryption for all data stored within these apps. This ensured that if a device was lost or stolen, the corporate data would remain secure and inaccessible.

2. Blocking Data Transfers:

One of Priya's top priorities was preventing sensitive information from leaking into personal apps. Alex configured the policy to:

- Block copying and pasting data between corporate and personal apps.

- Restrict saving files to personal storage locations, such as third-party cloud services.

"These settings keep work data where it belongs—inside Tenant B's ecosystem," Alex thought.

Alex turned his attention to access requirements, the rules that ensured only authorized employees could use these apps.

1. Requiring a PIN:

Alex set a policy that required users to enter a PIN each time they opened a corporate app. This simple measure added an extra layer of security, especially for devices without biometric authentication.

2. Conditional Data Wipe:

To address Priya's concern about inactive devices, Alex configured the policy to automatically wipe corporate data if a device didn't connect to Intune for 30 days.

"This way, even if someone forgets their work phone in a drawer for a month, the data won't sit there vulnerable," Alex noted.

Before rolling out the policy tenant-wide, Alex assigned it to a pilot group of 15 users across different departments. These employees used a mix of corporate-owned and personal devices, providing a representative test pool.

Testing Scenarios:

1. **Encrypting Data:** Alex sent a test email to his pilot group and asked them to save it locally in Outlook. He verified that the file was encrypted and inaccessible outside the app.

2. **Blocking Copy-Paste:** One employee attempted to copy text from a corporate email and paste it into a personal messaging app. The action was blocked, with a clear message: *"This action is restricted by your organization."*

3. **Access Requirements:** Alex tried to open OneDrive on a test device without entering the PIN. The app refused access until the correct PIN was provided.

4. **Data Wipe:** Alex manually simulated a 30-day disconnection scenario on a test device. At the end of the period, the policy successfully wiped all corporate data from the apps without affecting personal files.

With successful test results in hand, Alex deployed the policy to all users in Tenant B. He configured the deployment to roll out in phases over three days, ensuring the IT team could address any issues quickly.

To support employees during the rollout, Alex prepared a guide and FAQ that covered:

- The purpose of the policy.

- How to set up a PIN for corporate apps.

- What to do if they experienced restrictions, like blocked copy-paste.

Not all feedback was positive. During the rollout, Alex received an email from an employee who was frustrated by the restrictions on saving files to their personal cloud storage. The employee argued that this limitation made it harder to work from their personal laptop.

Alex scheduled a one-on-one meeting with the employee to explain the policy's purpose. "I get it," he said. "It's an adjustment. But this isn't about making your work harder—it's about protecting our data. If someone got access to your personal cloud, our sensitive information could be at risk."

To ease the transition, Alex suggested the employee use OneDrive's shared folders feature, which allowed them to collaborate securely without the need for personal storage. The solution worked, and the employee's concerns were addressed.

Alex monitored the policy's impact using the App Protection Status Dashboard in Endpoint Manager. Most users adapted quickly, but a few flagged issues prompted minor adjustments:

- **PIN Timeout:** Some employees requested a longer timeout period before being required to re-enter their PIN. Alex extended it from 15 minutes to 30 minutes for non-critical apps.

- **Copy-Paste Exceptions:** A specific finance tool required data transfer between Outlook and Excel. Alex added an exception for this app pairing to maintain workflow efficiency.

Once the policy was created, Alex saved it and assigned it to All Users in Tenant B's Azure AD.

Before rolling out the policy to all employees, Alex tested it on a personal phone he'd set up as an example BYOD device. The process involved:

1. **Installing Microsoft Apps:** Alex downloaded Outlook, Teams, and OneDrive from the app store.

2. **Signing In:** Using his test account, Alex signed into Outlook. The App Protection Policy was automatically applied.

3. **Testing Restrictions:**

    o   Alex tried copying text from a corporate email in Outlook and pasting it into a personal messaging app.

The action was blocked with a notification: *"Copying restricted by your organization."*

- o He attempted to save a OneDrive file to the device's local storage. The system enforced encryption, ensuring the file couldn't be accessed outside the OneDrive app.

The policy worked exactly as intended, protecting corporate data while leaving personal apps untouched.

With the policy tested and ready, Alex turned his attention to employee communication. He worked with Priya to draft a BYOD Usage Policy, which outlined:

- What IT could and couldn't access on personal devices.

- The steps employees needed to follow to enroll in the App Protection Policy.

- The benefits of the system, such as improved security and simplified app access.

To make the process even clearer, Alex created a short tutorial video walking employees through:

1. Downloading Microsoft apps from the app store.

2. Signing in with their corporate credentials.

3. Understanding the protections and restrictions applied by the policy.

The rollout began with a small pilot group of 10 employees. Alex monitored their feedback closely, addressing any concerns and fine-tuning the process as needed. One common question from the pilot group was: *"Will IT be able to see my personal emails or photos?"*

To address this, Alex emphasized the separation between corporate and personal data. "The policy only applies to the apps you use for work," he explained during a follow-up meeting. "Everything else on your device is completely private."

Once the pilot group's concerns were resolved, Alex expanded the rollout to the entire workforce. Employees received an email with the usage policy, a link to the tutorial video, and instructions for downloading the necessary apps.

As employees began enrolling their devices, Alex used the App Protection Status dashboard in Endpoint Manager to monitor adoption rates and address issues. The majority of employees enrolled without problems, but a few flagged devices needed additional troubleshooting:

- One user had an outdated version of iOS that didn't support the policy. Alex worked with Priya to notify the user about updating their device.

- Another user attempted to use an unsupported email app. Alex updated the policy's error message to include a list of approved apps, guiding users more effectively.

By the end of the week, Tenant B's App Protection Policy was fully deployed. Adoption rates were high, and employees appreciated the balance between security and privacy. Priya was thrilled. "This is exactly what we needed," she said during their wrap-up call. "Thanks for making it so smooth."

Notes:

This episode focuses on the foundational work for managing BYOD in Tenant B, highlighting how Alex uses App Protection Policies to secure corporate data while respecting employee privacy.

Key takeaways:

- **App Protection Policies:** Secure corporate data within specific apps without managing the entire device.

- **Testing:** Always test policies on a sample device before rolling them out to ensure they work as intended.

- **Employee Communication:** Clear usage policies and tutorials build trust and improve adoption rates.

- **Monitoring:** Use the App Protection Status dashboard to track enrollment and address issues quickly.

Strengthening Security: Conditional Access for Tenant B

Alex sat down with a fresh cup of tea, glancing at the open Conditional Access policy settings in Microsoft Endpoint Manager. The App Protection Policies for Tenant B were live, securing corporate data on personal devices. But data protection was only part of the equation. Alex's next challenge was to ensure that corporate resources—such as email, file storage, and the company intranet—were accessible only from compliant devices.

Conditional Access policies were like a security gate: they verified a user's device, compliance status, and identity before allowing access to sensitive resources. For a BYOD environment like Tenant B's, these policies were critical to maintaining control without disrupting productivity.

In a BYOD setup, devices are often a mix of corporate-owned and personal, spanning various operating systems, apps, and usage patterns. Conditional Access ensures that:

1. Only authorized users on secure devices can access company resources.

2. Personal devices meet minimum security standards, such as using approved apps and encryption.

3. Access is restricted to compliant browsers, reducing risks from third-party tools.

Tenant B relied heavily on three core resources that needed Conditional Access policies:

- Microsoft 365 (Email, Teams, and OneDrive).

- The HR Portal (SharePoint-based).

- The Finance Dashboard (Azure-hosted web app).

The hum of his laptop accompanied Alex as he leaned into another pivotal task for Tenant B: configuring a Conditional Access policy to secure access to Microsoft 365 apps. Priya had emphasized the importance of balance—enforcing strict security without frustrating employees. With a mix of personal and corporate devices in play, Alex needed to create a policy that ensured only compliant devices and approved apps could access corporate data.

"It's not just about keeping the bad actors out," Alex thought. "It's about making the process seamless for everyone who plays by the rules."

Alex logged into Microsoft Endpoint Manager, navigating to the Conditional Access within the Devices section. He clicked + New Policy, giving it a straightforward name: Secure Microsoft 365 Access.

As he worked through the configuration wizard, he selected All Users to ensure the policy applied across Tenant B's workforce. At the same time, he excluded service accounts to avoid disruptions to automated workflows.

"Conditional Access needs to enforce security without breaking everything else," Alex reminded himself. Excluding service accounts was a small but critical step to achieving that balance.

Alex turned his attention to defining the conditions under which users could access Microsoft 365 resources. He wanted to strike a balance between strong security and minimal disruption.
Alex added a condition requiring devices to be marked as compliant in Intune. This ensured that all devices accessing corporate resources adhered to the organization's baseline security policies, such as encryption and up-to-date software.
Next, Alex selected the option to limit access to approved apps. He included the core Microsoft 365 suite—Outlook, Teams, and OneDrive—and excluded unsupported apps that could pose security risks.
"This will help keep everything within our secure ecosystem," Alex thought as he reviewed the settings.

With the conditions in place, Alex configured the policy's enforcement actions. The goal was to block access from non-compliant devices or unsupported apps while providing clear instructions for remediation.

Alex set the policy to block access if a user attempted to sign in with a device that wasn't compliant with Intune policies. Similarly, any app that wasn't on the approved list would also be denied access. To reduce frustration, Alex created a custom error message to guide users who were blocked:

"Your device does not meet the security requirements to access Microsoft 365 resources. Please enroll your device in Intune or switch to an approved app. For assistance, contact Tenant B IT Support."

He knew that clear, actionable messages would reduce helpdesk tickets and make the transition smoother.

Alex applied the policy to a pilot group of 25 users. This group included employees from different departments and device scenarios—corporate laptops, BYOD tablets, and smartphones.

Testing Scenarios:

1. **Non-Compliant Device:** Alex tested a device that didn't meet Intune's compliance standards. The user was blocked, and the custom message provided clear instructions for enrolling the device.

2. **Unsupported App:** Alex attempted to log in using an unapproved email client. Access was denied, and the error message prompted the user to switch to Outlook.

3. **Compliant Device with Approved Apps:** On a fully compliant device, Alex opened Teams and successfully signed in, confirming that the policy didn't interfere with authorized workflows.

During the pilot, Alex received a complaint from a marketing employee who frequently used a third-party calendar app not on the approved list.

The employee was frustrated that the app no longer worked and felt it disrupted their workflow.

Alex scheduled a one-on-one session with the employee to explain the policy's purpose. "I get that this feels restrictive," he said. "But using approved apps ensures that our data stays secure, even if a device is compromised."

To address the concern, Alex explored whether the third-party app could integrate securely with Microsoft 365. When it became clear it couldn't meet Tenant B's security requirements, Alex suggested alternative workflows using Teams and Outlook's calendar integration.

By the end of the conversation, the employee was more understanding, and Alex logged the feedback to refine future communications.

With the pilot completed, Alex rolled out the policy to all users in Tenant B. To support the rollout, he prepared:

- A detailed FAQ addressing common questions about enrolling devices and using approved apps.

- A step-by-step guide for enrolling devices in Intune and ensuring compliance.

- A short training video demonstrating the secure sign-in process with Teams, Outlook, and OneDrive.

Once the policy was live, Alex monitored its impact using the Sign-In Logs in Azure AD. The logs provided insights into blocked sign-ins, helping Alex identify and address recurring issues:

- **Frequent Blocks from BYOD Users:** Alex identified a small subset of users who hadn't enrolled their personal devices. He reached out to them directly, guiding them through the process.

- **Unsupported App Attempts:** The logs revealed a handful of attempts to use unapproved email clients. Alex used this data to update the FAQ, emphasizing the importance of using Outlook.

Alex tested the policy on a non-compliant device by attempting to access email through a third-party app. The system blocked the attempt, displaying the custom error message:
"Access denied. Please enroll your device in Intune or use an approved app to access corporate email."

Satisfied with the results, Alex applied the policy to the rest of Tenant B.

The next step was to protect the SharePoint-based HR Portal, which housed sensitive employee information like payroll and benefits. The HR department had recently adopted a new, highly sensitive portal for managing employee records and payroll data. With the adoption came an urgent need for increased security. "We need to ensure only authorized HR staff can access the portal," Priya explained during their meeting. "And we need to make sure they're doing so securely."

Alex nodded, already envisioning the solution: a Conditional Access policy tailored specifically for the HR team. It would enforce stricter controls, requiring Multi-Factor Authentication (MFA) and ensuring access only from compliant devices or approved browsers. With his plan in mind, Alex opened the Conditional Access dashboard.

Alex clicked + New Policy and named it HR Portal Access. He knew the name needed to be clear and specific, as Tenant B's IT team would eventually manage and reference it.

In the Assignments section, Alex selected Users and Groups and targeted the HR Department group. This ensured the policy applied only to employees who needed access to the portal. To avoid disrupting system accounts, he excluded service accounts and administrative users who didn't interact with the HR portal.

"This way, we can focus the security measures exactly where they're needed," Alex thought.

Next, Alex moved to the Cloud Apps or Actions section and selected the HR portal as the protected app. He then configured the conditions that users needed to meet before gaining access:

1. Multi-Factor Authentication (MFA):

Alex required HR users to authenticate with MFA in addition to their standard credentials. "The sensitivity of this data demands an extra layer of security," Alex noted as he toggled the MFA requirement.

2. Device Compliance:

To ensure secure access, Alex added a condition requiring devices to be marked as compliant in Intune. This meant devices had to meet Tenant B's baseline security policies, such as encryption and up-to-date software.

3. Browser Restrictions:

Alex limited access to Microsoft Edge or compliant mobile apps, blocking outdated or unsupported browsers. He knew these restrictions would help prevent vulnerabilities often found in older browsers.

Before deploying the policy to the entire HR team, Alex assigned it to a pilot group of five HR employees. He wanted to ensure the configuration worked smoothly and identify any potential issues early.

Testing Scenarios:

1. **MFA Requirement:** Alex asked a pilot user to log into the HR portal from a compliant laptop. The system prompted the user for their password and a second authentication factor via Microsoft Authenticator. The process was seamless.

2. **Non-Compliant Device:** Alex tested access from a device missing encryption. The policy blocked access and displayed a message guiding the user to enroll their device in Intune.

3. **Unsupported Browser:** Alex attempted to log in using an outdated browser. The system denied access with an error message: *"Your browser is not supported. Please use Microsoft Edge or the HR mobile app."*

During testing, Alex encountered a challenge: a few HR employees were using outdated laptops that couldn't meet the compliance requirements. These devices lacked encryption and were running older versions of Windows.

The HR director expressed concern. "We can't disrupt their work while we figure out replacements," she said. "Is there a way to keep them online temporarily?"

To resolve the issue, Alex created a Temporary Exception Group in Azure AD. He added the non-compliant users to this group and configured a modified version of the HR Portal Access policy for them.

Modified Conditions:

1. Access was limited to specific tasks within the HR portal.

2. Users in the exception group were required to authenticate with MFA on every login.

3. The group was set to expire in 30 days, encouraging the affected employees to update their devices quickly.

"This isn't a long-term fix," Alex explained to the HR director. "But it ensures productivity while we address the compliance gap."

With the pilot successful and the exception group in place, Alex deployed the HR Portal Access policy to the entire HR team. He prepared a short onboarding guide explaining:

- How to enroll devices in Intune.

- Why MFA was now required for access.

- Supported browsers and apps for the HR portal.

To ensure a smooth transition, Alex hosted a virtual Q&A session with the HR department, addressing common concerns and walking users through the new login process.

After the rollout, Alex monitored the Sign-In Logs in Azure AD to track the policy's impact. The logs revealed:

- A sharp decline in unsupported browser attempts.

- A handful of users in the exception group who hadn't updated their devices yet.

To address the latter, Alex sent friendly reminders to those users, offering assistance with device updates and explaining the 30-day expiration of the exception policy.

The Finance Dashboard, hosted in Azure, was a critical resource for Tenant B's financial operations. It housed sensitive data that included budgets, payroll, and vendor contracts. Priya wanted extra assurances that ensure only authorized users could access it—and only under the most secure conditions.

Alex understood the importance of this request. With increased remote work and global access points, the dashboard's security had to account for more than just employee credentials. "It's time to lock this down," Alex thought, opening the Azure AD Conditional Access section in Microsoft Endpoint Manager.

The first step was targeting the right users. Alex navigated to Azure AD Groups and reviewed the Finance Group, which contained all employees who needed access to the dashboard. This ensured the policy would apply specifically to the group and wouldn't disrupt other departments.

"This makes sure we're protecting the right people while avoiding unnecessary disruptions," Alex thought as he saved the configuration.

The next step was verifying that every device accessing the dashboard met Tenant B's security standards.

Given the sensitivity of the data, Priya had requested additional restrictions to block unauthorized logins from outside approved locations. Alex added a location condition to the policy, allowing access only from approved countries where Tenant B operated.

1. Alex created a Named Location in Azure AD, listing the countries where Tenant B's employees were based.

2. He enabled the Block Access from Unapproved Locations option, ensuring any login attempts from outside these countries were automatically denied.

"This will help mitigate the risk of unauthorized international logins," Alex thought, adding a note to Priya to confirm the list of approved locations.

Alex assigned the policy to a pilot group within the Finance department to ensure everything worked as expected. He tested the policy with several scenarios:

1. **Compliant Device:** A test laptop enrolled in Intune with up-to-date encryption and OS versions successfully accessed the dashboard.

2. **Non-Compliant Device:** A test device missing encryption was denied access, with a custom error message directing the user to enroll their device in Intune.

3. **Blocked Location:** Alex simulated an international login attempt from an unapproved country. The policy blocked the attempt and flagged it in the Sign-In Logs as an unauthorized location.

During testing, a few employees in the Finance Group reported being blocked despite using compliant devices. After investigating, Alex discovered that their IP addresses weren't being recognized as part of the approved locations.

Alex updated the Named Location settings to include additional IP ranges for employees using corporate VPNs. He also configured a fallback policy that allowed VPN users to authenticate with Multi-Factor Authentication (MFA) as an added security measure.

Once updated, the policy worked seamlessly for the affected employees.

With the testing complete and the issues resolved, Alex deployed the Finance Dashboard Access policy to the entire Finance Group. To ensure a smooth rollout, he:

- Sent a detailed guide to employees explaining the new security measures and how to check their device compliance.

- Created a troubleshooting document for common issues, such as enrolling a device in Intune or updating its OS.

- Scheduled a virtual Q&A session for the Finance Group to address concerns and provide real-time support.

After the rollout, Alex monitored the Sign-In Logs in Azure AD to ensure the policy was functioning as intended. The logs provided valuable insights:

- **Blocked International Attempts:** A handful of login attempts from unapproved locations were flagged and blocked, confirming the location restrictions were effective.

- **Device Compliance Trends:** The logs showed a steady increase in compliant devices as employees updated their systems and enrolled in Intune.

Alex enabled logging for this policy, allowing Priya's team to monitor access attempts and flag any suspicious activity. This was especially important for finance-related data, which was a prime target for cyberattacks.

Once the Conditional Access policies were configured, Alex worked with Priya to notify Tenant B's employees about the changes. They sent an email outlining:

- The importance of the new policies in protecting company data.

- How to enroll devices or switch to approved apps if access was blocked.

- A link to the IT help desk for troubleshooting support.

To minimize confusion, Alex included examples of common scenarios, such as:

- *"What to do if you're blocked from accessing email on your phone."*

- *"How to install and use Microsoft Edge for accessing the HR Portal."*

As the policies rolled out, Alex kept a close eye on the Sign-Ins dashboard in Azure AD. This tool provided real-time insights into access attempts, including successful logins and blocked requests.

Observations:

- Most employees adapted quickly, with only a handful needing assistance to enroll their devices or update their apps.

- The number of blocked access attempts dropped significantly after the first week, indicating that employees were following the guidelines.

- Priya's team flagged one unusual login attempt from an unauthorized location. Alex reviewed the logs and confirmed it was a false positive caused by a VPN misconfiguration.

By the end of the rollout, Tenant B's Conditional Access policies were fully operational. Employees had secure access to the tools they needed, and Priya's team felt confident managing the new system. During their final call, Priya expressed her appreciation. "This has been a huge step forward for us," she said. "Thanks for making it happen."

Alex smiled. "You've got a great team, Priya. I'm excited to see how this system helps you grow."

Notes:

This episode dives into the details of configuring Conditional Access policies for Tenant B, providing step-by-step guidance on securing corporate resources in a BYOD environment.

Key takeaways:

- **Conditional Access for Microsoft 365:** Ensures employees use compliant devices and approved apps.

- **Role-Specific Policies:** Tailor Conditional Access settings to specific groups or resources, such as HR and Finance.

- **User Communication:** Clear instructions and examples help employees adapt to new access controls.

- **Monitoring:** Use the Azure AD Sign-Ins dashboard to track policy effectiveness and identify potential issues.

Refining Tenant B: Learning from Feedback and Fine-Tuning Policies

The flurry of activity in Tenant B's IT systems was a comforting sign to Alex as he logged into Microsoft Endpoint Manager. The App Protection and Conditional Access policies had been rolled out successfully, and the majority of employees were now securely accessing corporate resources. But Alex knew from experience that no deployment was truly complete until it had been tested in the real world and refined based on feedback.

This stage was where the nuances emerged—small adjustments that could improve usability, resolve unexpected issues, and ensure that Priya's team could manage the system with ease. Alex sipped his coffee, opened the feedback logs, and got to work.

The feedback from Tenant B's employees and IT staff had been mostly positive, but a few recurring themes stood out:

1. Some employees struggled to enroll their personal devices or access corporate apps.

2. A handful of devices were flagged as non-compliant due to minor issues.

3. There were requests for clearer error messages and better guidance during troubleshooting.

Alex began by tackling the first issue: simplifying the enrollment process for personal devices. He revisited the App Protection Policies to ensure the process was as user-friendly as possible.

The initial feedback highlighted confusion around enrolling personal devices into Intune. While the tutorial video had helped many employees, some were still unclear on the steps. Alex decided to make the process more intuitive by:

- **Updating the Enrollment Guide:** Alex revised the guide to include step-by-step screenshots and simplified language, walking employees through downloading Microsoft apps, signing in, and ensuring policies applied correctly.

- **Customizing Error Messages:** He updated the error messages for blocked access attempts, adding direct links to the updated guide and a contact email for IT support.

- **Improving Notifications:** Alex configured the App Protection Policy to send a push notification to employees whose apps were out of compliance, reminding them to update their settings.

Once the changes were in place, Alex tested the enrollment process on another BYOD device. This time, the updated error messages and notifications guided him seamlessly through the process, reducing the likelihood of confusion for employees.

Next, Alex turned his attention to the devices flagged as non-compliant. The Device Compliance dashboard revealed several common reasons for these flags:

1. Outdated operating systems on personal devices.

2. Missing app updates, causing apps like Outlook to fall out of compliance.

3. Encryption settings not fully applied.

For each issue, Alex took a targeted approach:

- **OS Updates:** Alex worked with Priya's team to notify employees whose devices needed OS updates, providing clear instructions and timelines for completing the updates.

- **App Updates:** He enabled App Update Policies in Endpoint Manager, automatically pushing updates for Microsoft apps to ensure compliance.

- **Encryption Settings:** For devices where encryption wasn't applied, Alex adjusted the policy to allow Intune to prompt users directly, walking them through enabling encryption.

After addressing these issues, Alex re-ran the compliance report. The number of flagged devices dropped by over 80%, a clear sign that the adjustments were working.

While the Conditional Access policies were functioning as intended, some users reported difficulty accessing specific resources, such as the HR portal or the Finance Dashboard. Alex revisited the policies to identify areas for improvement.

For the HR portal, Alex noticed that the location-based restriction was inadvertently blocking access for a small group of remote employees using VPNs. To resolve this, he:

- Updated the policy to recognize approved VPN IP ranges as compliant locations.

- Tested the policy on multiple devices to ensure it worked as expected.

For the Finance Dashboard, Alex found that one user was being flagged incorrectly due to a device name mismatch in Azure AD. He worked with Priya's team to update the device record, ensuring it reflected the correct compliance status.

As the system became more stable, Alex shifted his focus to empowering Priya's team. He scheduled a follow-up training session to cover:

- **Using the Compliance Dashboard:** How to monitor flagged devices, identify issues, and resolve them.

- **Managing Conditional Access Policies:** How to adjust rules as the organization's needs evolved.

- **Employee Support:** Tips for guiding employees through enrollment and troubleshooting.

During the session, Priya's team asked questions about edge cases, such as what to do if an employee's device was repeatedly flagged as non-compliant. Alex recommended using Device Compliance Alerts in Endpoint Manager to proactively notify IT about recurring issues, allowing them to address problems before they disrupted workflows.

With the refinements complete, Alex invited feedback from both employees and Priya's team. He sent a brief survey asking:

- How easy it was to enroll devices and access resources.

- Whether error messages and guidance were clear.

- Any additional suggestions for improvement.

The responses were overwhelmingly positive, with employees appreciating the balance between security and usability. One comment stood out: *"I was worried about IT taking control of my phone, but this system feels invisible—it just works."*

Priya's team also expressed confidence in their ability to manage the system moving forward. "This has been a huge learning experience for us," Priya said during their final call. "We're in a much better place now than we were a month ago."

By the end of the week, Tenant B's Intune environment was running smoothly. Compliance rates were high, access issues were minimal, and employees were adapting well to the new policies. Alex sent Priya a summary of the refinements:

Hi Priya,

I'm thrilled with the progress we've made on Tenant B's Intune environment. The refinements have significantly improved compliance rates and resolved the access issues flagged during the rollout.

Your team has done a fantastic job adapting to the new system, and I'm confident you'll continue to build on this foundation. Let me know if there's anything else I can support you with as you settle into the system.

Best,
Alex

Notes:

This episode highlights the importance of refining a system based on real-world feedback, emphasizing the need for ongoing adjustments and training.

Key takeaways:

- **Enrollment Process:** Simplify and guide employees through BYOD enrollment to reduce confusion.

- **Compliance Management:** Address common issues with targeted solutions, such as automatic app updates and proactive notifications.

- **Policy Refinement:** Revisit and adjust Conditional Access rules based on user feedback and unique scenarios.

- **Training and Empowerment:** Equip IT teams with the tools and knowledge they need for long-term success.

Enrolling Devices in Windows Autopilot for Tenant C

Alex sat back in his chair, reviewing the notes for Tenant C's deployment. This tenant was a blank slate, offering the rare opportunity to set up a modern Intune environment from scratch. The first step was to enroll Tenant C's devices into Windows Autopilot, ensuring every device—whether new or existing—could be provisioned with minimal IT involvement.

Autopilot wasn't just about convenience. It was a cornerstone of modern device management, allowing IT teams to deploy devices remotely with pre-configured settings and apps. For Tenant C, it would transform how they onboarded devices, saving time and creating a consistent experience for employees.

Alex glanced at the mix of devices in Tenant C's inventory. While some were new enough to support Autopilot out of the box, others would require manual configuration. He took a deep breath and began working through the enrollment process.

Windows Autopilot is a tool that simplifies device provisioning by automating the setup and configuration process. Instead of imaging devices manually, IT teams can use Autopilot to:

- Pre-configure settings, apps, and policies before a device is handed to the user.

- Allow users to set up devices themselves by signing in with their corporate credentials.

- Ensure every device meets compliance requirements right out of the box.

For Tenant C, Alex planned to use two methods to enroll devices into Autopilot:

1. **Hardware Hash Method:** For devices not currently enrolled in Azure AD.

2. **Convert Targeted Devices to Autopilot:** For existing devices already enrolled in Intune.

For new and unregistered devices, the hardware hash is a unique identifier that connects the device to Autopilot. Alex worked with Ethan, Tenant C's IT admin, to collect and upload these hardware hashes to Intune.

Alex used a simple Powershell script to extract the hardware hash from each device:

md c:\HWID

Set-Location c:\HWID

Get-WindowsAutoPilotInfo -OutputFile AutoPilotHWID.csv

o The script created a CSV file containing the hardware hash, ready for upload.

Then Alex uploaded that list of hardware hashes into Intune.

o In the Microsoft Endpoint Manager Admin Center, Alex navigated to Devices > Enroll Devices > Windows Enrollment > Devices.

o He uploaded the CSV file and verified that the devices appeared in the Autopilot list.

The hardware hash method is ideal for onboarding new devices or those that haven't been registered in Azure AD. It ensures they're linked to Tenant C's Intune environment before being handed to employees.

With Autopilot successfully deployed for new devices, Alex turned his attention to a pressing task: bringing existing devices into the fold. While new devices could be pre-enrolled in Autopilot during procurement by working with the vendor at the time of purchase, many of Tenant B's laptops were already in use, running Windows 10 or later. Claire had emphasized the importance of consistency. "If all devices follow the same Autopilot profiles, it'll make life easier for both IT and employees."

Fortunately, Microsoft Endpoint Manager offered a way to convert compatible devices into Autopilot without requiring a hardware hash—a process Alex was eager to leverage.

Alex logged into Microsoft Endpoint Manager and navigated to the Devices section. From there, he filtered the enrolled devices to display only those running Windows 10 or later. These operating systems supported the Autopilot conversion process, eliminating the need for complex manual configurations.

The list included dozens of laptops and desktops currently in use across Tenant C. Alex exported the list to double-check details like device names, owners, and compliance status, ensuring there were no surprises during the conversion.

"This list will help us focus on devices that are ready for Autopilot without unnecessary complications," Alex thought, noting a few older systems that would require a different approach.

With the target devices identified, Alex returned to Endpoint Manager and created a group of test devices. He knew it was critical to validate the process on a smaller scale before rolling it out tenant-wide.

•

In the Microsoft Intune admin center, Alex navigated to Devices > Windows > Windows enrollment > Deployment Profiles. He created a new profile. Within the profile settings, he located the option labeled "Convert all targeted devices to Autopilot" and set it to Yes. Next, he assigned the Autopilot deployment profile to the group containing the devices he wished to convert. Alex knew that once the profile was assigned, Intune would initiate the process of capturing the hardware hashes of the targeted devices and adding them into Autopilot.

"This is much faster than the manual method," Alex thought as the test devices successfully registered for Autopilot.

Ethan had emphasized two key goals during their last meeting: "We need consistency and simplicity. Whether it's a new hire or a device reset, the setup process should feel intuitive and professional." With those goals in mind, Alex set to work on designing a configuration profile that met Tenant C's specific needs.

Tenant C operated across multiple regions, but Ethan wanted every device to start with the same defaults for Wi-Fi, language, and region. Alex adjusted these settings in the profile:

- **Wi-Fi Configuration:** Alex preloaded the credentials for Tenant B's secure Wi-Fi network, ensuring that devices automatically connected during the setup process.

- **Language and Region Defaults:** He set the language to English (US) and the region to the United States, reflecting the primary operating location of Tenant B.

"Employees shouldn't have to fiddle with these settings," Alex noted. "They should just work."

One of Ethan's top priorities was reinforcing Tenant C's identity during the setup process. Alex navigated to the Company Branding section and uploaded the following:

- **Logo:** A high-resolution version of Tenant B's logo, which would appear prominently on the login screen.

- **Color Scheme:** A custom color palette featuring Tenant B's signature blue and white tones.

The branding transformed the previously generic Windows login screen into a polished, professional interface that reflected Tenant C's culture.

"This little touch makes a big difference," Alex thought, previewing the branded setup screen. "It's the first thing employees see, and it reinforces the company's identity."

The final step was configuring the profile to preload the apps employees used daily. Alex navigated to the Apps section of Endpoint Manager and created a list of required software:

- **Microsoft 365 Apps:** Including Word, Excel, PowerPoint, and Outlook.

- **Microsoft Teams:** The backbone of Tenant B's communication.

- **OneDrive:** Essential for file storage and collaboration.

Alex assigned these apps to the Autopilot group, ensuring they would automatically install during the setup process. "Employees should log in and get to work without worrying about installing the basics," Alex thought as he finalized the configuration.

Before rolling out the profile tenant-wide, Alex tested it on a handful of devices. He selected a mix of new laptops and reset older devices to simulate various scenarios.

Testing Checklist:

1. **Wi-Fi Connection:** Devices connected automatically to the secure network during setup.

2. **Language and Region:** The defaults worked flawlessly, requiring no user intervention.

3. **Branded Login Screen:** The logo and color scheme displayed correctly, creating a professional first impression.

4. **Preloaded Apps:** Once setup was complete, all core apps were installed and ready to use.

Everything worked perfectly, though Alex noticed the app installation process took longer than expected on one older device. After some investigation, he optimized the deployment by prioritizing smaller apps during the initial setup and scheduling larger apps like Teams for a second wave.

With the testing complete, Alex assigned the profile to all new and converted devices in Tenant C. He also updated the onboarding guide for employees, highlighting how the Autopilot experience streamlined setup.

Ethan was thrilled when he saw the branded login screen and preloaded apps in action. "This is exactly what we needed," he said. "It's professional, intuitive, and saves everyone so much time."

By the end of the rollout, every device in Tenant C followed the same setup process, creating a unified experience for employees and simplifying IT management. For Alex, the project demonstrated how thoughtful configuration could blend security, efficiency, and company culture into a seamless whole.

Alex applied the profile to the converted devices and rebooted one of them for testing. As the device restarted, it seamlessly entered the Autopilot deployment flow, applying the assigned settings and apps without requiring manual intervention.

"This will make onboarding and re-deploying these devices so much simpler," Alex noted.

Before rolling out the conversion tenant-wide, Alex conducted a series of tests to ensure the process worked as expected:

1. **Device Reboot:** Alex confirmed that converted devices automatically applied the Autopilot profile during the next restart.

2. **User Experience:** He logged in as a test user to verify the preloaded apps and settings were functional.

3. **Compliance Monitoring:** Alex checked the compliance status of the converted devices in Intune, ensuring they adhered to Tenant B's security policies.

Confident in the results of the test group, Alex expanded the process to include all compatible devices in Tenant C. To streamline the conversion, he divided the rollout into phases:

- **Phase 1:** Convert devices used by IT staff, ensuring they could troubleshoot any potential issues.

- **Phase 2:** Expand to devices in critical departments like Finance and HR.

- **Phase 3:** Complete the conversion for all remaining devices.

During Phase 2, Alex encountered an issue with a few devices that failed to convert. After investigating, he discovered these devices hadn't synced with Intune recently due to outdated OS versions.

Alex worked with Ethan's IT team to push OS updates to the affected devices via Endpoint Manager. Once updated, the devices synced successfully and completed the Autopilot conversion process.

To minimize confusion, Alex prepared a user-friendly guide explaining what employees could expect after their devices were converted to Autopilot. The guide covered:

- How the login process would change.

- What apps and settings would be preloaded.

- Troubleshooting tips for common issues, like connecting to Wi-Fi during the setup phase.

He also sent out a brief email notification before each phase of the rollout, giving employees a heads-up about the changes.

Once the rollout was complete, Alex monitored the converted devices using the Autopilot Deployment Reports in Endpoint Manager. The reports provided insights into:

- Deployment success rates.

- Devices requiring additional configuration or troubleshooting.

- Employee feedback collected via a follow-up survey.

By the end of the process, Tenant C's devices were fully integrated into the Autopilot system, providing a unified experience for both employees and IT. Ethan was delighted. "This is going to save us so much time during re-deployments," she said. "The consistency across devices is a huge win."

For Alex, the project highlighted the power of modern management tools to simplify even the most complex tasks. "When technology works like this," he thought, "it's a win for everyone."

This approach eliminates the need to manually collect hardware hashes for devices already in Intune, streamlining the process for existing hardware.

To ensure Ethan and his team could manage Autopilot independently, Alex provided hands-on training. The session covered:

- How to collect and upload hardware hashes for new devices.
- Using the "Convert to Autopilot" feature for existing devices.
- Assigning and updating Autopilot profiles in Intune.
- Monitoring enrollment progress in the Intune dashboard.

By the end of the session, Ethan felt confident. "This is exactly what we've needed," he said. "I can't wait to start using this for all our new hires."

Notes:

This episode breaks down the process of enrolling devices in Windows Autopilot, showing how Alex tailored the setup for Tenant C's mix of new and existing hardware.

Key takeaways:

- **Hardware Hash Method:** Ideal for enrolling new or unregistered devices into Autopilot.
- **Convert to Autopilot:** Streamlines the process for devices already enrolled in Intune.
- **Autopilot Profiles:** Customizing profiles ensures a consistent and user-friendly setup experience.
- **Training:** Empowering IT teams to manage Autopilot independently is critical for long-term success.

Configuring Compliance Policies for Tenant C

With Tenant C's devices successfully enrolled in Windows Autopilot, Alex turned his attention to the next critical step: configuring compliance policies. These policies would act as the foundation of Tenant C's security posture, ensuring that every device met baseline standards for encryption, operating system updates, and password complexity. For a team as small and resourceful as Tenant C's, a streamlined, manageable compliance framework was key.

Alex opened the Microsoft Endpoint Manager Admin Center and began drafting the policies that would secure Tenant C's devices while maintaining flexibility for legacy hardware.

Compliance policies define the rules a device must follow to be considered secure. In an Intune environment, these policies:

- Protect corporate data by enforcing encryption and security standards.

- Block non-compliant devices from accessing sensitive resources via Conditional Access.

- Provide IT admins with visibility into device health and security risks.

For Tenant C, Alex planned to create a baseline compliance policy that covered:

1. Operating system requirements.

2. Encryption standards.

3. Password complexity.

4. Support for older devices with limited hardware capabilities.

Alex began by creating a baseline compliance policy that would apply to all devices enrolled in Tenant C's Intune environment. He navigated to

Devices > Compliance Policies > Create Policy and selected Windows 10 and later as the platform.

Configuring Policy Rules:

1. **Operating System Requirements:**

   o Devices must run Windows 10 version 20H2 or later.

   o Alex configured the policy to block devices running older versions but allowed a 14-day grace period for updates.

2. **Encryption Standards:**

   o All devices were required to use BitLocker encryption.

   o Alex enabled a compliance rule that flagged devices without encryption and notified users to enable BitLocker.

3. **Password Complexity:**

   o Alex set a rule requiring passwords to be at least eight characters long, with a mix of uppercase, lowercase, numbers, and symbols.

   o He configured a 90-day expiration policy to ensure passwords were updated regularly.

4. **Device Health Checks:**

   o Alex enabled rules to verify that Windows Defender was active and up-to-date on all devices.

Tenant C's inventory included several older devices that couldn't meet the baseline requirements, particularly for BitLocker encryption. To accommodate these devices while maintaining security, Alex created an exception group in Azure AD.

1. Alex created a new group in Azure AD named "Legacy Devices Exception Group."

2. He added devices that couldn't support BitLocker or other compliance rules to this group.

3. In the compliance policy, Alex added an exception for the Legacy Devices group, allowing them to pass compliance checks while flagging them for eventual replacement.

For devices in the exception group, Alex applied alternative security measures:

- Enabled encryption using third-party tools where BitLocker wasn't supported.

- Set stricter password policies to offset the lack of hardware encryption.

Before rolling out the compliance policy to all devices, Alex tested it on a pilot group. He selected five devices, including both modern and legacy hardware, to ensure the policy worked as intended.

1. A modern device with BitLocker enabled: Passed compliance checks with no issues.

2. A device running an outdated OS: Flagged as non-compliant, with a notification prompting the user to update.

3. A legacy device in the exception group: Passed compliance due to the exception but was flagged for monitoring.

During testing, Alex noticed that one device took longer than expected to apply BitLocker. He updated the policy to send users a follow-up notification if encryption wasn't enabled within 24 hours.

With the testing complete, Alex deployed the compliance policy to all devices in Tenant C. He divided the rollout into phases:

1. **Corporate-Owned Devices:** These were enrolled first to ensure the baseline rules were applied.

2. **BYOD Devices:** These followed, with a focus on enforcing app protection and access restrictions rather than full device compliance.

Alex monitored the rollout using the Device Compliance dashboard in Endpoint Manager. The majority of devices reported as compliant within the first 48 hours, with a few exceptions that required manual intervention.

To ensure employees understood the importance of compliance policies, Alex worked with Ethan to draft a notification email. The email included:

- A summary of the new compliance rules.

- Steps for resolving non-compliance issues, such as enabling BitLocker or updating the OS.

- A link to the IT support team for additional help.

Alex also created a short troubleshooting guide for employees, addressing common issues like:

- "What to do if my device is flagged as non-compliant."

- "How to enable BitLocker encryption."

- "How to update Windows to the latest version."

As the policy rollout progressed, Alex used the compliance dashboard to identify and address recurring issues. For example:

- **Outdated Drivers:** A few devices were flagged due to outdated network drivers, which Alex resolved by pushing driver updates through Intune.

- **Unencrypted Devices:** For devices that didn't enable BitLocker automatically, Alex worked with Ethan to troubleshoot encryption errors and ensure compliance.

By the end of the week, compliance rates had reached over 95%, with only a handful of legacy devices remaining in the exception group.

The compliance policies were now fully operational, providing Tenant C with a secure foundation for device management. Alex sent Ethan a summary of the progress:

Hi Ethan,

The compliance policies are now live, and I'm happy to report a compliance rate of over 95%. The exception group for legacy devices is working well, and we've resolved most flagged issues.

Let me know if you need help with further refinements or monitoring as you settle into the new system. Great work so far!

Best,
Alex

Notes:

This episode focuses on building and deploying compliance policies for Tenant C, highlighting how Alex balances security with flexibility to accommodate legacy devices.

Key takeaways:

- **Baseline Compliance Policies:** Set minimum standards for OS updates, encryption, and passwords.

- **Exception Groups:** Accommodate older hardware while planning for eventual replacement.

- **Testing:** Test policies on a small group of devices to identify and resolve issues early.

- **User Guidance:** Provide clear notifications and troubleshooting resources to support employees.

Simplifying App Deployment and Updates for Tenant C

With Tenant C's compliance policies in place and functioning smoothly, Alex's next priority was ensuring employees had seamless access to the applications they relied on. For a small team like Tenant C's, application deployment wasn't just about installing software—it was about creating a system that minimized IT overhead while keeping apps up to date and secure.

Alex opened the Client Apps section in Microsoft Endpoint Manager. He reviewed Tenant C's app requirements, which included essential productivity tools like Microsoft 365, Microsoft Teams, and a proprietary scheduling app. With a clear plan in mind, he began configuring app deployment policies.

In modern IT environments, app deployment through Intune offers several key benefits:

- **Centralized Management:** Apps are deployed and updated automatically, reducing manual work for IT teams.

- **User Productivity:** Employees have access to the tools they need, configured with minimal setup.

- **Security:** Ensures apps are always up to date, reducing vulnerabilities from outdated software.

For Tenant C, Alex aimed to strike a balance between required apps, which would install automatically, and optional apps, which employees could download on demand through the Company Portal.

Required apps are those that every employee needs to perform their job. For Tenant C, this included:

- Microsoft 365 (Word, Excel, PowerPoint, Outlook).

- Microsoft Teams for collaboration.

- A VPN client for secure remote access.

In Endpoint Manager, Alex navigated to Apps > All Apps > Add App and selected Microsoft 365 Apps (Windows 10 and later). He customized the deployment settings. First he selected only the desktop versions of Word, Excel, PowerPoint, and Outlook to minimize storage impact. Then he enabled automatic updates to ensure apps stayed current. Finally, he assigned the app to All Devices, ensuring every enrolled device received it automatically.

For Teams and the VPN client, Alex repeated the process, targeting the All Devices group to standardize deployments across the organization.

Alex added a test device to the deployment group and verified that the required apps installed automatically. Within minutes, Word, Excel, and Teams were ready to use, pre-configured with Tenant C's branding and settings.

Optional apps, like Tenant C's proprietary scheduling software, didn't need to be installed on every device. Instead, Alex made them available through the Company Portal, allowing employees to download them as needed.

Alex added the scheduling app to Apps > All Apps > Add App and uploaded the installation package provided by Ethan's team. He assigned the app to the Available for enrolled devices group, making it visible in the Company Portal. Then he customized the app's description in the portal, including a brief overview of its features and a link to user documentation.

Alex opened the Company Portal on a test device, ensuring the scheduling app appeared correctly and installed without issues. The process was straightforward, and Alex knew employees would appreciate the flexibility it offered.

Keeping apps up to date was critical for both security and productivity. Alex configured Intune to handle updates automatically, reducing the burden on Tenant C's IT team. For Microsoft 365 apps, Alex enabled Update Management in the deployment settings, ensuring new versions were applied during off-peak hours. For the scheduling app, Alex created an App Update Policy that pushed updates as soon as a new version was available. He scheduled a weekly app update report in Endpoint Manager, allowing Ethan to monitor the status of deployed updates.

To validate the update process, Alex pushed a minor update to the scheduling app. Within minutes, the updated version appeared on the test device, confirming the system worked as intended.

To ensure a smooth rollout, Alex worked with Ethan to draft a communication plan for Tenant C's employees. The email included:

- A list of required apps that would install automatically.

- Instructions for accessing optional apps through the Company Portal.

- A reminder to leave devices powered on during scheduled update windows.

Alex also created a short tutorial video walking employees through the Company Portal, demonstrating how to find and install apps.

As the app deployment policies rolled out, Alex used the App Install Status dashboard in Endpoint Manager to monitor progress. Most devices reported successful installations, but a few flagged errors due to:

1. **Insufficient Storage:** Some older devices lacked the storage space for Microsoft 365 apps.

   o Alex worked with Ethan to identify these devices and recommend storage upgrades.

2. **Network Issues:** A few remote devices experienced download failures due to weak Wi-Fi connections.

   o Alex configured the deployment policy to retry installations automatically when network conditions improved.

By addressing these issues proactively, Alex ensured that the deployment stayed on track.

Finally, Alex conducted a training session for Ethan and his team, covering:

- How to add new apps to the Intune environment.

- Monitoring app deployment and update status in Endpoint Manager.

- Troubleshooting common issues, such as failed installations or update errors.

Ethan was impressed by how intuitive the system was. "This is going to save us so much time," he said. "I can't believe we were doing all of this manually before."

By the end of the rollout, Tenant C's app deployment process was running smoothly. Employees had access to the tools they needed, and Ethan's team felt confident managing updates and new deployments. Alex sent a summary email to Ethan:

Hi Ethan,

The app deployment policies are live and working well. All required apps have been installed, and the Company Portal is fully operational for optional apps. Let me know if you'd like help refining anything or adding new apps in the future.

Best,
Alex

Notes:

This episode explores the process of configuring app deployment and updates for Tenant C, showcasing how Alex simplifies IT management while improving the employee experience.

Key takeaways:

- **Required Apps:** Automatically deploy critical apps to all devices for consistency.

- **Optional Apps:** Use the Company Portal to give employees flexibility while maintaining control.

- **App Updates:** Automate updates to ensure apps remain secure and functional.

- **Training:** Empower IT teams to manage app deployments independently.

Configuring and Testing VPN Access for Tenant C

With app deployment complete, Alex shifted his focus to a critical aspect of Tenant C's environment: VPN access for remote employees. Tenant C relied on a VPN to connect users to on-premises resources, including file shares and proprietary systems. For many employees, this connectivity was the backbone of their daily workflows.

Alex knew the VPN setup had to be seamless. Employees needed to connect securely without navigating complex configurations. At the same time, IT needed a reliable way to monitor and troubleshoot connections. Armed with this goal, Alex opened the Microsoft Endpoint Manager Admin Center and began planning.

During discovery, Alex had documented Tenant C's VPN needs:

1. **Pre-Configured Profiles:** Employees should not have to manually input server information or authentication settings.

2. **Always-On VPN:** Certain roles required the VPN to connect automatically whenever the device accessed corporate resources.

3. **Split Tunneling:** To optimize bandwidth, only corporate traffic should route through the VPN.

Alex also noted the VPN solution in use—Azure VPN Gateway—and confirmed its compatibility with Intune's VPN configuration options.

Alex began by setting up a VPN profile that would be deployed to all devices. He navigated to Devices > Configuration Profiles > Create Profile in Endpoint Manager and selected Windows 10 and later > Templates > VPN. For connection type Alex selected IKEv2, as recommended by Tenant C's VPN provider. He then entered the server address provided by Ethan's team. Alex configured the profile to use certificate-based authentication for added security. He uploaded the root certificate for Tenant C's VPN and assigned it to the profile. Next, Alex enabled split tunneling to route only corporate traffic through the VPN.

95

For employees requiring constant connectivity, Alex created a second profile with Always-On settings, targeting a specific group in Azure AD.

To ensure the profile worked as expected, Alex deployed it to a pilot group of 10 devices, including both on-premises and remote setups. Once the profile was pushed, Alex worked through a series of test scenarios:

- **Scenario 1: First-Time Connection:**
  Alex reset a test device to simulate an employee setting up the VPN for the first time. Upon login, the device automatically connected to the VPN using the pre-configured settings.

- **Scenario 2: Split Tunneling Verification:**
  Alex opened a corporate intranet site and confirmed the traffic routed through the VPN. Then, he accessed a public website to verify it bypassed the VPN.

- **Scenario 3: Always-On Connectivity:**
  Alex tested a device in the Always-On group by simulating a network drop. The VPN reconnected automatically once the device regained internet access.

The tests were largely successful, though one remote device experienced slower connection speeds due to an outdated network driver. Alex flagged the device for an update.

While monitoring the test deployment, Alex encountered two common issues:

1. **Certificate Errors:** One device failed to connect due to a missing certificate. Alex resolved this by reassigning the certificate profile in Intune and confirming it applied correctly.

2. **User Authentication Failures:** A few employees in the pilot group mistyped their credentials during the first login attempt. Alex updated the deployment guide to include a step-by-step walkthrough for signing in.

Once the pilot group's issues were resolved, Alex prepared to roll out the VPN profile to all devices. He divided the deployment into two phases:

1. **Corporate-Owned Devices:** These were prioritized to ensure the core workforce had secure access.

2. **BYOD Devices:** Alex configured a separate VPN profile for BYOD users, requiring them to install the Company Portal app and enroll their devices in Intune before receiving the VPN configuration.

To ensure smooth operations post-rollout, Alex conducted a training session with Ethan and his team. The session covered:

- **Monitoring VPN Connections:** How to use the VPN Status Dashboard in Intune to track connected devices and troubleshoot issues.

- **Managing Certificates:** Best practices for renewing and deploying certificates to avoid authentication errors.

- **Supporting Employees:** Tips for guiding users through common scenarios, such as resetting VPN connections or updating credentials.

Ethan appreciated the clear instructions. "This will definitely help us stay on top of things," he said. "I feel like we've got a good handle on this now."

To ensure employees understood the new VPN setup, Alex and Ethan drafted an email announcement. The email included:

- A summary of the new VPN configuration and its benefits.

- Instructions for using the VPN, including login details and troubleshooting tips.

- A link to the IT support team for further assistance.

Alex also recorded a short tutorial video demonstrating how to connect to the VPN and access corporate resources. The video was shared via the Company Portal, making it easy for employees to refer back to it.

As the VPN profile rolled out across Tenant C's devices, Alex monitored its performance in Endpoint Manager. The majority of devices connected successfully, but a few flagged issues required intervention:

- **Unstable Connections:** Two remote devices experienced intermittent drops due to weak Wi-Fi signals. Alex recommended network upgrades to the affected employees.

- **Authentication Timeouts:** One employee reported delays during login, which Alex traced back to a slow DNS server on the user's ISP. He added a fallback DNS configuration to the VPN profile to resolve the issue.

With the VPN configuration fully deployed, Tenant C's remote employees were securely connected to on-premises resources. Ethan's team felt confident managing the system, and Alex prepared to wrap up his work on this tenant.

He sent Ethan a summary email to mark the milestone:

Hi Ethan,

The VPN profile is now live, and the rollout has been a success. Most devices are connected and functioning as expected, with only minor issues flagged during monitoring. Your team did a great job supporting the deployment, and I'm confident you'll handle any future updates with ease.

Let me know if you need help with anything else as you settle into the new system. Thanks again for your collaboration!

Best,
Alex

Notes:

This episode focuses on configuring and deploying a secure VPN solution for Tenant C, highlighting the importance of testing, troubleshooting, and communication.

Key takeaways:

- **Pre-Configured VPN Profiles:** Simplify the user experience while ensuring secure connectivity.

- **Always-On VPN:** Critical for roles requiring constant access to corporate resources.

- **Testing and Monitoring:** Pilot deployments help identify and resolve issues before scaling.

- **Training and Communication:** Empowering IT teams and employees ensures a smooth rollout.

Tenant A: The Balancing Act of Hybrid Complexity

Alex sat back in his chair, his laptop glowing with the familiar dashboard of Microsoft Endpoint Manager. Tenant A had been the most complex of the three environments he had worked on. Their reliance on a hybrid Active Directory infrastructure, combined with legacy dependencies, presented unique challenges.

He had a call scheduled with Claire, Tenant A's IT director, to review the results of the project. As he waited for the meeting to start, Alex reflected on the path they had taken to modernize Tenant A's device management.

Tenant A's environment had been a mix of old and new. On-premises Active Directory coexisted with a growing Azure AD footprint. Devices ranged from brand-new Windows 11 laptops to older machines that hadn't seen an update in years. Claire's team relied heavily on legacy systems that weren't cloud-friendly, and these systems added layers of complexity to their hybrid setup.

"Hybrid environments are like patchwork quilts," Alex had joked during one of their initial planning meetings. "Beautiful when they come together, but every piece needs careful stitching."

The core challenge had been enabling seamless integration between their legacy systems and modern cloud-based management tools. Intune's capabilities were robust, but they required meticulous configuration to function smoothly alongside Tenant A's existing infrastructure.

The first hurdle had been ensuring all devices—both new and existing—were enrolled in Intune. For devices already on the network, Alex leveraged Group Policy Objects (GPOs) to automate enrollment. The process worked well for most devices, but a handful of them resisted compliance due to mismatched User Principal Names (UPNs) in Azure AD and on-prem AD.

"This mismatch is like giving someone the wrong phone number and wondering why they don't call," Alex had explained to Claire. The fix involved updating the affected accounts in Azure AD to align with the on-prem naming conventions. Once resolved, those devices enrolled seamlessly.

With devices enrolled, the next step was creating a set of compliance policies to standardize security across Tenant A's environment. Alex focused on three key areas:

1. **Encryption:** Requiring BitLocker for all Windows devices.

2. **Updates:** Enforcing a minimum OS version and regular update checks.

3. **Password Policies:** Strengthening password requirements to reduce vulnerabilities.

During testing, Alex discovered that several older laptops couldn't enable BitLocker due to outdated hardware. He worked with Claire to flag these devices as exceptions, scheduling them for replacement during the next budget cycle. In the meantime, he added additional protections, such as restricting access to sensitive apps from these devices.

One of Claire's priorities was ensuring employees had immediate access to core applications like Microsoft Teams, Outlook, and OneDrive. Alex configured App Deployment Policies in Intune, targeting security groups for different departments.

The deployment worked smoothly for most users, but Claire flagged an issue: her finance team reported missing applications on their laptops. After some investigation, Alex discovered that the finance group hadn't been added to the correct Azure AD security group. "An easy fix," Alex said, updating the group membership and pushing the apps to the affected devices.

Perhaps the most delicate task was securing Tenant A's legacy systems. These systems used older protocols that weren't natively supported by Azure AD. To bridge the gap, Alex configured Hybrid Azure AD Join for these devices, ensuring they could authenticate to both the cloud and on-prem resources.

To protect access to the legacy systems, Alex implemented Conditional Access policies that restricted access to compliant devices and enforced Multi-Factor Authentication (MFA). This step dramatically improved security while maintaining compatibility.

As the meeting with Claire began, Alex reviewed the final outcomes with her:

- **Enrollment Success:** Over 95% of devices were now enrolled and compliant with Intune policies.

- **Security Enhancements:** Conditional Access policies and updated compliance requirements significantly reduced vulnerabilities.

- **Legacy Compatibility:** All critical legacy systems were securely accessible through the hybrid setup.

Claire was thrilled. "We've been trying to untangle this mess for years," she said. "Now it feels like we finally have control."

Notes:

Tenant A's journey showcased the challenges of modernizing a hybrid environment while maintaining legacy compatibility. The key to success lay in balancing the old and new—leveraging modern tools like Intune while respecting the limitations of existing systems.

Key takeaways:

- **UPN Alignment is Critical:** Hybrid environments rely on consistent identities across on-prem and cloud systems.

- **Flagging Exceptions is OK:** Legacy devices may not meet every compliance standard, but temporary exceptions can maintain productivity while planning for replacements.

- **Conditional Access is a Game-Changer:** Restricting access to compliant devices ensures security without disrupting workflows.

Tenant B: Navigating the BYOD Landscape

Alex sipped his coffee and opened his laptop to review the results of the latest policy rollout. Tenant B had presented a completely different set of challenges compared to Tenant A. While Tenant A focused on hybrid complexity, Tenant B operated in a BYOD-first environment where employees used personal devices to access corporate resources.

Priya, the IT Director at Tenant B, had one major concern: balancing security with usability. "Our people love their devices," she had said during their first meeting. "We need security that works with them, not against them."

BYOD environments are inherently tricky. Personal devices can't be fully managed like corporate-owned hardware, but they still need to meet security standards when accessing sensitive resources. For Tenant B, the priority was clear: protect corporate data while respecting user privacy.

Alex's task was to implement Mobile Application Management (MAM) policies through Intune. These policies would isolate corporate data within approved apps, ensuring that sensitive information stayed protected, even on unmanaged devices.

Alex started by creating App Protection Policies in Intune. These policies would enforce security at the app level, rather than the device level, giving Tenant B the flexibility it needed.

Key Settings in the Policy:

1. **Data Encryption:** Alex ensured that all data within corporate apps, such as Outlook and Teams, was encrypted.

2. **Copy-Paste Restrictions:** To prevent data leakage, Alex blocked copying and pasting between corporate apps and personal apps.

3. **Save Restrictions:** Employees could only save files to OneDrive for Business, blocking third-party cloud storage services.

As Alex tested the policies, he used his own personal device to simulate the user experience. Opening a corporate email in Outlook, he tried copying text into a personal messaging app. A notification appeared: *"This action is restricted by your organization."*

"Perfect," Alex thought. "It's strict, but the message makes it clear why."

Next, Alex layered Conditional Access policies on top of the app protections. These policies ensured that only compliant devices and approved apps could access Tenant B's Microsoft 365 resources.

Key Conditional Access Rules:

1. **Approved Apps Only:** Access to resources like Outlook, Teams, and OneDrive was limited to the official Microsoft apps, blocking third-party alternatives.

2. **Device Compliance:** Alex required devices to meet basic security standards, such as having a passcode and running the latest OS updates.

3. **Risk-Based Access:** To enhance security further, Alex enabled Conditional Access to block risky sign-ins, such as those flagged for unusual activity or login attempts from unfamiliar locations.

During the policy rollout, Alex encountered resistance from some employees who were hesitant to enroll their personal devices in Intune. "I don't want IT looking at my private data," one user said during a feedback session.

To address these concerns, Alex and Priya held a company-wide virtual town hall to explain the policies. Alex emphasized that:

- Intune's MAM policies only managed corporate apps and data, leaving personal apps untouched.

- IT would not have access to personal photos, messages, or other private information on employees' devices.

106

- The policies were designed to protect the company's data, not spy on employees.

After the town hall, Alex created an FAQ document that answered common questions and alleviated misconceptions. This transparency helped win over the majority of users.

To ensure the policies worked as intended, Alex conducted extensive testing with a pilot group. The group included employees from different departments who used a variety of devices, including Android phones, iPads, and personal laptops.

Testing Scenarios:

1. **Non-Compliant Device:** Alex tested an older smartphone without a passcode. The device was blocked from accessing Outlook, with a message guiding the user to enable a passcode.

2. **Copy-Paste Restrictions:** A test user tried to paste text from Teams into a personal note-taking app. The action was blocked as expected.

3. **Approved Apps Only:** Alex attempted to log into OneDrive using a third-party app. Access was denied, with a clear notification to use the official Microsoft app.

One unexpected issue arose during the rollout: a small group of users relied on an unsupported third-party email app that didn't comply with the Conditional Access policies. These users expressed frustration, arguing that switching to Outlook disrupted their workflow.

Alex met with Priya to discuss the issue. They decided to create a temporary exception group, allowing these users limited access while they transitioned to Outlook. Alex also worked with the IT team to offer personalized training sessions, helping employees make the switch smoothly.

"Change is always hard," Priya said, "but we'll get there."

With the pilot successful and user concerns addressed, Alex rolled out the policies to the rest of Tenant B. The deployment included:

- A quick-start guide for enrolling devices and accessing corporate apps.

- Video tutorials demonstrating how to use Teams, Outlook, and OneDrive under the new policies.

- Regular check-ins with Priya to monitor progress and gather feedback.

By the end of the rollout, Tenant B's BYOD environment was significantly more secure. Employees could access corporate resources with confidence, knowing their personal data remained private. Priya was impressed. "You've made this transition so much smoother than I expected," she said.

For Alex, the project highlighted the importance of communication and transparency in securing BYOD environments. "It's all about building trust," he thought. "When people understand why policies exist, they're more willing to adapt."

Notes:

Tenant B's story illustrates the unique challenges and opportunities of managing BYOD environments. The combination of app protection, Conditional Access, and transparent communication created a secure yet user-friendly solution.

Key takeaways:

- **MAM Policies Protect Data Without Managing Devices:** This approach is ideal for BYOD environments where privacy is a concern.

- **Conditional Access Adds Another Layer of Security:** Limiting access to compliant devices and approved apps reduces risks.

- **Transparency is Key:** Clear communication and user education help overcome resistance to new policies.

Tenant C: Scaling Simplicity for a Remote-First Workforce

Alex adjusted his headset as his call with Ethan, Tenant C's IT lead, began. "We're not as complicated as the other tenants," Ethan joked, "but we're growing fast. I need something simple that works now and will scale as we add more people."

Tenant C's fully remote workforce posed unique challenges. Employees worked from all over the country, often on varying devices. Unlike Tenant A's hybrid infrastructure or Tenant B's BYOD-heavy policies, Tenant C needed a straightforward system that ensured security, simplified onboarding, and could handle rapid expansion.

"Simplicity is the ultimate sophistication," Alex replied. "Let's focus on building a foundation that's easy to manage but can grow with you."

Tenant C's needs were clear:

1. **Streamlined Onboarding:** Every new hire needed a consistent setup experience, regardless of their location or device.

2. **Secure Access:** Protect sensitive data with minimal disruption to the user experience.

3. **Future-Proofing:** Ensure the system could handle a growing workforce without requiring constant IT intervention.

Alex's plan focused on leveraging Windows Autopilot, Intune, and Conditional Access to deliver a seamless experience for Tenant C's employees while giving Ethan's lean IT team the tools they needed to scale.

The first step was creating an Autopilot Deployment Profile tailored to Tenant C's needs. Alex designed the profile to streamline the setup process, ensuring new devices were pre-configured with the apps and settings employees needed.

111

- **Standardized Configuration:** Settings for Wi-Fi, language, and time zone were preloaded to reduce user input during setup.

- **Preloaded Applications:** Microsoft 365 apps, Teams, and OneDrive were automatically installed.

- **Minimal IT Interaction:** Devices were shipped directly to employees and configured through Autopilot without requiring hands-on setup by the IT team.

Alex piloted the profile on a few test devices. He simulated the new hire experience by resetting the laptops and running them through the Autopilot setup. Within minutes, the devices were configured, branded, and ready to use.

"This is exactly what we need," Ethan said when he saw the results. "Fast, consistent, and zero hassle."

Tenant C's remote setup required robust security measures that didn't interrupt productivity. Alex configured Conditional Access policies to ensure secure access to Tenant C's resources.

Key Policy Settings:

1. **MFA Requirement:** Employees were required to authenticate using Multi-Factor Authentication (MFA) for all Microsoft 365 logins.

2. **Device Compliance:** Only devices enrolled in Intune and meeting security standards were allowed access.

3. **Geo-Restrictions:** Alex blocked logins from outside approved locations, reducing the risk of unauthorized access.

To help users understand security requirements, Alex added clear error messages to guide employees through remediation steps if their devices were blocked. "Simple communication is key," he thought as he tested the policy.

Tenant C relied on a handful of essential applications, but employees often needed access to additional tools based on their roles. Alex used Intune App Assignment to streamline app deployment:

- **Core Apps:** Preloaded for all users during setup.
- **Role-Based Apps:** Assigned dynamically based on Azure AD groups, such as Marketing, Finance, or IT.

This approach ensured employees had everything they needed without overwhelming their devices with unnecessary apps.

Tenant C's rapid expansion meant onboarding new employees every week. To keep up with the pace, Alex created a scalable onboarding process:

1. **Automated Workflows:** Autopilot profiles and Intune policies ensured new devices were configured automatically.
2. **Self-Service Portals:** Employees could request additional apps or access permissions through a user-friendly portal.
3. **Training Resources:** Alex developed short videos and guides to help employees navigate their new devices and tools.

"This system can handle 10 new hires or 100 without breaking a sweat," Alex explained during a final review with Ethan.

With the deployment complete, Alex used Endpoint Manager's Device Compliance Dashboard to monitor the rollout. The dashboard provided real-time insights into device status, policy compliance, and potential issues.

Alex noted that a small percentage of devices were flagged for missing updates. He worked with Ethan to push a remediation policy, ensuring those devices met compliance standards within 24 hours.

By the end of the rollout, Tenant C's remote workforce was fully equipped with secure, consistent devices. Employees logged in from across the country, enjoying a seamless experience that allowed them to focus on their work.

Ethan couldn't have been happier. "This is the most efficient system we've ever had," he said. "It's simple, scalable, and exactly what we needed to grow."

Notes:

Tenant C's story highlights the power of simplicity in IT management. By focusing on streamlined processes and scalable solutions, Alex was able to meet the needs of a fast-growing remote workforce.

Key takeaways:

- **Autopilot Streamlines Onboarding:** Pre-configured profiles save time and reduce IT workloads.

- **Conditional Access Protects Data:** Security doesn't have to be disruptive when policies are well-designed.

- **Scalability is Key:** Automated workflows and self-service portals ensure IT can keep up with growth.

Closing the Loop: Reflections and Next Steps

The familiar buzz of a Teams notification pulled Alex's attention to his screen. It was time for the final closeout meeting with Claire, Priya, and Ethan—the IT leads for Tenants A, B, and C. Over the past few months, Alex had helped each tenant navigate their unique challenges, implementing tailored Intune and Autopilot solutions that modernized their environments.

As Alex clicked the meeting link, he felt a mix of accomplishment and anticipation. The project had been a journey, but this was the moment to reflect on what worked, what didn't, and how each tenant could continue to evolve.

"Good afternoon, everyone," Alex began, his voice steady. "It's been a privilege to work with each of you. Today, I want to review our progress, address any remaining concerns, and discuss how you can continue to build on the systems we've implemented."

Claire from Tenant A, Priya from Tenant B, and Ethan from Tenant C all appeared on-screen, their expressions a mix of satisfaction and curiosity.

"We've come a long way," Claire said, setting the tone. "Tenant A is finally seeing the benefits of modern management, even with our hybrid setup."

Priya nodded in agreement. "And our BYOD policies have made a huge difference for Tenant B. The employees were skeptical at first, but now it's second nature."

Ethan chimed in. "Tenant C is running like a well-oiled machine. We've onboarded 15 new hires in the past month without a hitch."

Alex started with Tenant A, sharing the key outcomes:

- Over 95% of devices were enrolled and compliant with Intune policies.

- Hybrid Azure AD Join bridged the gap between legacy systems and modern management.

- Conditional Access significantly improved security without disrupting workflows.

Claire was quick to praise the progress but raised a lingering concern. "Our legacy systems are still a pain point. What's the best way to phase them out?"

Alex suggested a phased approach:

1. **Audit Legacy Systems:** Identify critical applications and prioritize updates or replacements.

2. **Leverage Azure Virtual Desktop (AVD):** Host remaining legacy apps in a secure cloud environment to minimize dependencies.

3. **Set a Timeline:** Create a roadmap for fully transitioning to modern, cloud-native tools.

"This isn't an overnight change," Alex said. "But the foundation is there. You're already ahead of where you were six months ago."

Next, Alex turned to Tenant B, where the focus had been on balancing security with usability in a BYOD-heavy environment.

Key achievements included:

- App Protection Policies isolated corporate data while respecting user privacy.

- Conditional Access restricted access to approved apps and compliant devices.

- Transparent communication eased employee concerns about device enrollment.

Priya raised a challenge they had recently faced. "A handful of employees are still resistant to using Intune. How do we get them on board?"

Alex emphasized the importance of continued education and flexibility:

1. **Host Interactive Q&A Sessions:** Encourage employees to share concerns and provide live demonstrations of the system.

2. **Highlight Success Stories:** Share examples of how the policies have improved security and productivity.

3. **Enforce Gradual Adoption:** Set clear deadlines for compliance but offer temporary exceptions for valid use cases.

"Resistance is normal," Alex said. "But with time and transparency, you'll win most of them over."

For Tenant C, simplicity and scalability had been the guiding principles. Alex recapped the progress:

- Autopilot streamlined onboarding for new hires.

- Conditional Access ensured secure remote access for all employees.

- Self-service portals empowered employees to request additional apps or permissions.

Ethan had a question about future growth. "We're adding another 50 employees next quarter. Is there anything else we should do to prepare?"

Alex recommended the following:

1. **Expand Automation:** Use Intune's dynamic groups to automatically assign apps and policies based on roles.

2. **Monitor Trends:** Regularly review Intune's dashboards to identify and address emerging issues.

3. **Document Processes:** Create a comprehensive onboarding guide to maintain consistency as the team grows.

"You've built a scalable system," Alex said. "Now it's about maintaining and optimizing it."

As the meeting neared its end, Alex encouraged each IT lead to share their reflections on the project.

Claire from Tenant A spoke first. "This project taught us the value of patience and persistence. Modernizing a hybrid environment isn't easy, but it's worth it."

Priya from Tenant B added, "For us, it was all about trust. Once employees understood the why behind the policies, adoption became much easier."

Ethan from Tenant C smiled. "Sometimes, keeping it simple is the smartest move. Autopilot and Intune just work."

Alex nodded, summarizing their insights. "Each of you faced unique challenges, but the principles of modern management—simplicity, security, and scalability—applied across the board. I'm confident you're set up for success."

Before wrapping up, Alex outlined a few next steps for each tenant:

- **Tenant A:** Begin transitioning legacy systems and exploring Azure Virtual Desktop for legacy app hosting.
- **Tenant B:** Continue building trust with employees and refining BYOD policies as needed.
- **Tenant C:** Focus on maintaining scalability and preparing for future growth.

As the meeting concluded, Priya spoke for the group. "Alex, you've been an incredible partner throughout this process. Thank you for guiding us every step of the way."

Alex smiled, grateful for the opportunity to make an impact. "This has been a team effort," he replied. "If you ever need support in the future, you know where to find me."

Notes:

This episode brings the project full circle, highlighting the unique challenges, solutions, and growth for each tenant. It reinforces the importance of tailoring IT strategies to meet specific organizational needs while reflecting on the shared principles that drive success.

Key takeaways:

- **Adaptability is Key:** Each tenant required a unique approach, but the core principles remained the same.

- **Communication Builds Trust:** Transparent communication fosters collaboration and smoother adoption of new policies.

- **IT is Never Finished:** Modern management is an ongoing process that requires regular monitoring and optimization.

As you finish this book, if you are keen to deepen your knowledge of Intune, you have several options:

- Supplement your learning with other books in the Intune Playbook Companion Series

- Contact Dr. Patrick Jones for information about professional service opportunities at www.AuditSolv.com

- Check out the online Intune Basics course provided by Olympus Academy, which includes detailed instructions and video tutorials.

Bit.ly/intunebasics

Thank you for supporting this publication and enjoy your learning!

www.ingramcontent.com/pod-product-compliance
Lightning Source LLC
LaVergne TN
LVHW022351060326
832902LV00022B/4386